John Matthews & Charles Newington

The Goblin Market Tarot

"Up the airy mountain and
down the rushy glen
We daren't go a-hunting for
fear of little men."

*William Allingham,
The Fairies*

Dedication

To all those who visit the Goblin Market.

"Thus go the faery kind,

Whither Fate drives them; not as we

Who fight with it, and deem ourselves free [...]

For to them Fate is the Lord of Life."

Euripides, Hypsipyle

The Goblin Market Tarot
John Matthews & Charles Newington

First published in the UK and USA in 2021 by
Watkins, an imprint of Watkins Media Limited
Unit 11, Shepperton House, 83–93 Shepperton Road
London N1 3DF

enquiries@watkinspublishing.com

Design and typography copyright © Watkins Media Limited 2021
Text copyright © John Matthews 2021
Artwork copyright © Charles Newington 2021

The right of John Matthews to be identified as the Author of this text
has been asserted in accordance with the Copyright, Designs and
Patents Act of 1988.

Commissioning Editor: Fiona Robertson
Editor: Kelly Thompson
Editorial Assistant: Brittany Willis
Designer: Lee-May Lim
Production: Uzma Taj

A CIP record for this book is available from the British Library
ISBN: 978-1-78678-554-1

10 9 8 7 6 5 4 3 2 1

Printed in China

www.watkinspublishing.com

Contents

Introduction

"O benign divinity of places, bestow upon us eyes and hearts such as will recognise the hidden shrines all over the world and within every lane's turning; and grant us, as thy highest boon, to wander every now and then in *The Enchanted Woods*, between the hour of rising from our solitary work and the hour of sitting down to meat with our dear friends!"

Vernon Lee, The Enchanted Woods

Welcome to the World of Faery

It has never been safe to go into the realm of Faery. If you are unfortunate enough to stray into it (or fortunate, depending on how you look at it) you have to take care. If you eat their food or drink their water, you can find yourself stuck there for a thousand years — during which time you will grow no older. But if and when you find your way back into this world, you will very likely turn to the dust of ages the moment your feet touch the earth. In the poem that forms the basis for this tarot, you can see why they were rightly feared.

The realm of Faery is ultimately mysterious. It has been known about, explored and its denizens encountered for a very long time. Only recently it has become the home of tinsel-winged, twinkling beings who supposedly grant wishes and that have little effect on our world. This tarot is not about them. Rather than the sweetly sentimental beings of the Victorian era, or the even more cloyingly creations of more recent times, we are looking back to an older era, when the people of Faery were seen for what they are: dangerous, tricky, and rightly suspicious of us.

They mostly come out at twilight. A rustle under the hedge, a glimmer of light from the darkness beneath the trees, a whisper as dusk advances. Now you see them; now you don't. They can be kind or cruel, beautiful, or ugly, large or small, noble or ignoble. They are mostly found in wild places — under trees or bushes, inside hills or beside streams. They seem utterly unknowable, and they have many names: Peri, Volkers, Twlyth Teg, Elves, Pixies, Korrigans, Merrows, Greenies, Jinni, the Sidhe. Goblins are a little different, being made more of earth than sky as the more widely viewed faeries are. But they are still people of Faery, ruled over by the King and Queen of that realm. So, for goblins, read faeries — just as Christina Rossetti, the author of the enchanting poem which inspired us to create this deck, did. But they all fall within the realm of Faerie.

Faeries are often glamorous — in fact our modern word for a beautiful person comes from an older word: 'glamour' which once meant a spell cast upon a mortal so that they were irresistibly drawn to a faery, like a moth to a flame. In the Scottish story of Tam Lin, a young man called True Thomas falls in love with a Queen of Faery and becomes her slave, unable to escape for many years until a mortal girl who loves him wins him back by undergoing terrible tests in which she must hold onto him as he shapeshifts from human to animal, fish and red-hot iron. In the world of the Goblin Market, the races you will encounter are both

beautiful and strange. You will find gorgeous fasces and figures next to strange, wrinkled, twisty forms.

The idea of a faery market varies widely in folk lore and personal reminiscence. The Goblin Market conjured up by Christina Rossetti is very different to the more traditional style yet retains a great deal of the same lore. On the surface the goblins are seen as mischievous, tricky, even dangerous — but while this is typical of faery lore, Rossetti uses it to show the problems of human interference in faery matters. One of the best accounts of the sighting of an *actual* faery market is by English author Richard Bovet, dating from 1684. Having visited communities in Somerset, he recorded what he had been told by local residents:

"The place near which they most ordinarily showed themselves was on the side of a Hill, named Black Down, between the parishes of Pitminster and Chestonford, not many miles from Taunton. Those that have had occasion to travel that way have frequently seen them, appearing like men and women, of a stature generally near the smaller size of men. Their habits used to be of red, blue or green, according to the old ways of country garb, with high-crowned hats. One time about 50 years since, a person living at Combe St Nicholas, a parish lying to one side of that hill, near Chard, was riding towards his home that way, and saw, just before him, on that side of the hill, a great company of people, that seemed to him like country folk

assembled at a fair. There were all sorts of commodities, to his appearance, as at our ordinary fairs; pewterers, shoemakers, pedlars, with all kinds of trinkets, fruit and drinking booths [...] At length it came to his mind what he had heard concerning the fairies on the side of that hill, and it being near the road he was to take, he resolved to ride in amongst them, and see what they were. Accordingly he put on his horse that way, and though he saw them perfectly all the long as he came, yet when he was up on the place where all this had appeared to him, he could discern nothing at all, only seemed to be crowded and thrust as when one passes through a throng of people. All the rest became invisible to him until he came to a little distance, and then it appeared to him again as at first."

This account keeps with faery tradition in that humans tend to catch mere *glimpses* into the Faery world, with things vanishing from sight once we draw near — although we may still *feel* their presence brushing or jostling against us, as in this account. Ultimately, faeries are almost synonymous with the word mysterious.

It's safe to say that faeries are an old race. Some think they are an ancient memory of an older people that once lived on the surface of the earth thousands of years ago but were driven underground by invaders from across the seas. This is why we hear about them living in caves or vast mazes of tunnels where mortals go at their peril. Others will tell you that the faeries are the old, pagan

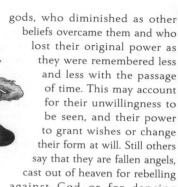

gods, who diminished as other beliefs overcame them and who lost their original power as they were remembered less and less with the passage of time. This may account for their unwillingness to be seen, and their power to grant wishes or change their form at will. Still others say that they are fallen angels, cast out of heaven for rebelling against God or for dancing on a Sunday.

Nobody quite agrees about faeries; and perhaps that's just as well. A world without them would be a sadder, colder place. Think of Peter Pan's famous question: *"Do you believe in Faeries?"* — asked in countless theatres full of children there to see J. M. Barrie's great play. The answer to this question, shouted back from generations of children, is always: *"Yes!"* And that's how it should be — and not only for children. Faeries enrich our lives with magic and the lure of the unknown. This is why we made *The Goblin Market Tarot*.

The *Goblin Market* Poem

While most Victorian accounts of faery tend to be sentimental – wrapped in twinkle and tinsel – the *Goblin Market* poem, written by the young Christina Rossetti in 1862 and which you'll find a compete text of at the end of this book (see pages 169–189), is a shining exception to this in that it shows us a world of faery that is very far from the conventional expectations of winged beings, decorously living their tiny lives.

Instead, she shows us a faery world that is challenging and dangerous. A world from which you might not return should you venture in – at least not without being changed forever. A world in which the faeries – mostly goblins (the foot soldiers, if you will, of the Faery Kings and Queens) – are quite savage creatures, as far from the Tinkerbells of modern times as we can possibly get. And yet these goblins also carry a strange wisdom, offering us a glimpse into a world that – whether or not we believe in its existence – offers some remarkable visions.

The goblins here are wheedling, mocking and assaulting – with cat, snail and wombat faces. They deal in tempting fruit, which we see one sister desire and one avoid. They make up their own rules and change them according to how they feel, breaking into the lives of the sisters and changing them forever. Their physicality is shocking, unexpected and seemingly amoral. There is nothing safe or comfortable about them. Instead, they come across as urgent, insightful beings who erupt into life on the page, lashing their tails, clawing and jostling for attention.

The poem tells the story of two sisters — one of whom (Laura) goes into Faery and samples the fruity delights of the Goblin Market only to suffer the consequences, and the other (Lizzie) remains behind, trying to help her sister. It shows us the dangers of accepting forbidden fruits — something that has been warned against since ancient times.

The allegorical nature of the poem is very clear, with the lesson being not to "go down to the woods today" because, if you do, you'll be in trouble! It's a parable that we find again and again in Victorian literature — all about the dangers of getting mixed up with unsuitable men, as this would all too often lead to unwanted pregnancy and despair. The poem lays it on heavily, along with what now seems like clearly erotic symbolism.

The description of the relationship between the two girls, although couched in Victorian imagery as a natural closeness between siblings, has made the work something of a Sapphic favourite and has turned the author into a gay icon — a notion that would almost certainly have horrified its devoutly Christian author.

The Author of the Poem:
Christina Rossetti (1830–1894)

Christina Rossetti — author of *Goblin Market* among many other poems — was born in 1830, the daughter of political exile Gabriele Rossetti and his half-English, half-Italian wife, Frances Polidori. Her brother was the tempestuous artist and poet Dante Gabriel Rossetti, a co-founder of the Pre-Raphaelite Brotherhood.

It is a testament to her memory that, of her many poems, the two that people tend to remember most are *Goblin Market* and the one used as the lyrics for the carol *In the Bleak Midwinter*. Almost Gothic in style due to its spikey and at times disturbing imagery, *Goblin Market* was acclaimed as a great success when first published in 1862, despite art critic John Ruskin's slighting mention in a review of her unusual and innovative metre, which is what, in my opinion, drives the poem.

Christina's early influences were books like *The Arabian Nights* and Thomas Keightley's *Fairy Mythology*. However, as she grew older, she was drawn into a group within the Church of England known as the Tractarian Movement, and so began to gravitate to Anglo-Catholic spirituality of a particularly pious kind. These two poles of influence are highly apparent when reading her poetry, for she seems to combine a passionate nature with a life of self-abnegating constriction, in which she chose an almost nun-like existence, while also serving for a time as a volunteer at a charitable institution for the reclamation of "fallen women".

The sisters in Christina's *Goblin Market* poem could be seen to combine the two halves of her *own* nature: Lizzie who rejects the luscious fruit, and Laura who indulges in the goblin's fruit. On one level, it is the story of a child rapt away to Faeryland, and on the other, it is a much more subtle tale of redemption through sisterly love.

Weaving through the poem are many images of the fruit that the goblins are purveying. It has been argued that the fruit is a metaphor for sexuality, but it could equally represent opium, especially since her brother's wife, Lizzie, lived the last part of her life in a laudanum haze, eventually dying from an overdose in 1862.

The first edition of the poem bore a frontispiece by her brother, Dante Gabriel Rossetti, which showed Laura succumbing to the goblins' wheedling, while the title page depicted the two sisters asleep in bed, "golden head by golden head". The goblins were shown here as animal-headed beings with human hands, and in Christina's personal copy of the manuscript, there are watercolours in the margins depicting the goblins as athletic figures dressed in blue who are half-animal, half-human. Perhaps these part-animal depictions were inspired by Christina's regular visits to Regent's Park Zoo, in London, which enchanted her. The presence of a blind wombat next to a porcupine there led her brother to purchase a wombat for her, which sat on her table over dinner and once ate a whole box of cigars!

Christina's *Goblin Market* poem had a great deal of influence on others, including American poet Emily Dickinson, whose mention of goblins in her short gnomic poems began after the publication of the first American edition of Christina's poem in 1864. It is also thought that William Allingham's poem, *The Faeries*, quoted at the start of this book, was inspired by Christina's poem.

Many editions of the *Goblin Market* poem have been illustrated by well-known artists — from Arthur Rackham, known for his illustration of *Grimm's Fairy Tales* to Charles Vess, known for his work on early ballads, themselves filled with faery characters.

Feminist critics have looked to Christina's position as the youngest daughter in the family — who was usually not expected to marry, in order to be able to nurse her ageing parents — as an explanation for her sense of self-sacrifice over her gifts as a writer, despite which she published a considerable amount of poetry. She seems to have possessed somewhat of a sense of unworthiness, which was, no doubt, also fostered by the general lack of expectation around women's achievement during that era. It is also clear to note, with feminist hindsight, how the goblins in her poem have a predatory role, while the burden of *moralistic* life falls upon the sisters — very much like the situation of the women having to compete in the Victorian marriage market of the time.

Christina Rossetti died in 1894, after suffering with breast cancer. William Sharp, the writer of the popular *Immortal Hour* fairy opera, regarded her as "the finest woman-poet since Mrs Browning" (Elizabeth Barrett Browning).

The Goblin Market Deck and Artwork

In creating this divinatory version of the poem, we set out to reflect the energy and underlying sadness of the poem, laced with the rather aggressive focus of the goblins themselves, along with a dash of humour which is also present in the original — though well hidden. Our deck is not just goblin — it includes the faery races of which they are a part and draws upon the history of these beings as recorded from the middle ages. Thus, we have a Faery King and Queen and other strange creatures, not all of which are included in the poem. We do, of course, have plenty of the luscious magical fruit which is mentioned so often in the text and which seems always to suggest the risk of eating faery food — a prohibition against which is well recorded in folk lore.

The usual process through which I go when devising a new tarot is to come up with ideas and brief the artist to what I can imagine. Not so with this one. I sent Charles a list of titles both major and minor trumps and began to receive batches of images in a matter of days. These were so right that I was amazed. There were echoes of Fuseli and Blake, but Charles' inimitable wit and wisdom shone from them. These were not so much illustrations as portraits of a kind I had never seen before. I was certain that I was looking at *real* fairies, goblins and the like. Once I began to write this book, I realised that I was being told a story, a story about a faery who visits our world — very different to the more usual intent of us going there in search of knowledge. As work on the deck progressed, I saw that this story reflected our human hopes and desires, making it a unique view into the role of Faery in our own imaginations. The Faery Wanderer (see Card 0) invites us into his world, and into the amazing vision of the Goblin Market. It is a vision we have done our best to replicate, as clearly as possible, for others to see.

A Special Symbol to Watch Out For

You may notice a symbol that appears throughout all the cards — sometimes small, sometimes large, sometimes just one, sometimes multiple — that of a small spiral with a downward bisecting line.

This is an ancient image, particularly associated with the Sidhe, the faery people of Ireland — and signifying a gateway into their world. It became central to my 2004 book *The Sidhe: Wisdom from the Celtic Otherworld* and has since threaded through many of my other works. So look out for this symbol as you use the deck and see if it adds to your experience of working with *The Goblin Market Tarot*.

PART 1

Getting to know *The Goblin Market Tarot*

The Major Arcana

In this section you will find out about the faery goblins who replace the traditional archetypes of the first 22 cards (the Major Arcana) in *The Goblin Market Tarot*:

Goblin Market Card Names	Traditional Card Names
0: The Faery Wanderer	The Fool
1: The Cunning Man	The Magician
2: The Enchantress	The High Priestess
3: The Faery Queen	The Empress
4: The Faery King	The Emperor
5: The Faery Wiseman	The Hierophant
6: The Faery Lovers	The Lovers
7: The Faery Wagon	The Chariot
8: The Faery Switch	Justice
9: The Lone Faery	The Hermit
10: Fortune's Rule	The Wheel of Fortune
11: The Secret Way	Fortitude
12: The Upsodowner	The Hanged Man
13: The Dark One	Death
14: The Faery Dreamer	Temperance
15: The Faery Trickster	The Devil

16: The Fallen Tree	The Tower
17: The Starry Roof	The Star
18: The Moonlit Spell	The Moon
19: The Sun Room	The Sun
20: The Queen's Favour	Judgement
21: The Faery Realm	The World

Some of the Goblin Market card names will be unfamiliar. Some derive from characters who appear in the *Goblin Market* poem and some from the larger world of Faery. Thus, the Cunning Man, the Faery Queen and the Faery Switch, for example, all come from traditional tales; while others, such as the Lone Faery, the Upsodowner and the Starry Roof, are names inspired by the poem or derived from folklore traditions.

The best way to get to know the cards is to sit with them for a while, holding the deck loosely in your hands, with eyes closed, then taking one card at a time and studying it carefully. Notice the symbols, the colours, the numerical shaping of some cards (especially the Minors), the presence of the fruits and other wares offered at the Goblin Market. Remember that you are tuning into the essence of the place (which is between worlds and realities) and the beings whose wisdom you are able to access via the cards and through your own intuition.

For each of the Major Arcana cards, you will find firstly some background information about the faery/goblin archetype in hand, as well as, more often than not, the traditional tarot archetype to which it relates.

You will then find "Divinatory Insights" to help you craft your readings. These insights should never replace the meanings you find for yourself after spending time with the cards; they are here simply to offer you inspiration for your own interpretations if you feel you need or want them.

Below the insights you will then find two sets of "Goblin Whispers" that give the key themes relating to each card:

- the "Upside" themes: the main associations for the cards that emerge *upright* in readings;
- the "Downside" themes: associations for the cards that emerge from the deck reversed i.e. upside-down.

These words of "Upside" and "Downside" guidance from the muttered voices of the goblins are glimpses into a much larger world, but are no less powerful for that. If you are in need of a swift response when you do a reading, look to these. Then follow them with the more detailed interpretations when you have more time; you will notice that the more detailed interpretations for all the cards — both Major and Minor — also generally *start* with the Upside reading and *end* with the "on the Downside" reading.

Remember that, as with all tarot decks, the cards themselves have no magical power. They are made up of symbols that offer glimpses into the other worlds that surround us. So look out for those symbols — not just the ones that are mentioned in the explanations in the pages that follow, but also the ones that go *un*mentioned — the ones that you find for yourself, where much faery gold waits to be discovered.

Read the cards with care and treat them well. Be willing to go past the *surface* of the images you see on them, be open to the transformational messages within them, and let their shared wisdom reach your heart and mind and spirit.

O: THE FAERY WANDERER

The Fool is one of the most ancient characters. Here named the Faery Wanderer, he challenges the establishment, bursts the balloon and moves at his own pace — an explorer who sets out on a great journey ignorant but with a willingness to learn.

Jack, the eternal simpleton of faery tale, is a type of Fool, as is Perceval, the Grail winner in Arthurian legend. He is the comedic clown of ancient Greek drama, the simpleton of Shakespeare's darkest plays, Merlin in his madness, and the shaman of Irish myth, Suibhne Gelt.

There are not many fools in Faery. The denizens of Faery are mostly cleverer than us, and frequently make *us* look foolish. But there are a few who decide to explore *our* world. To them, it seems, the dimension that we occupy is every bit as strange and mysterious as theirs is to us. So, when a lone faery decides to cross the bridge between one realm and the other, stepping off into space with the Apple of Knowledge in his hand, surrounded by strange creatures and filled with expectations, we may follow where he leads. Those who do so will learn a great deal about their own journeys.

Because he is outside normal reality, the Faery Wanderer has no number. His ability is not only to represent you, the seeker, but also to lead the way for you, moving throughout the deck and changing, like a chameleon, whenever he encounters one of the other archetypes. You might see him as a blank page, waiting for words to be written that will explain his journey. He beckons you to follow, and stands at a point of beginnings, of fresh starts, of trusting life to take you where you need to be.

Here, the Faery Wanderer begins his journey without prior thought, launching himself into an adventure that may lead anywhere. Innocent and sometimes foolhardy, he is filled with determination to discover the truth. This may lead some to walk where others cannot or will not go, stepping off into space without concern, in the belief that they will find a new sense of reality through determination alone.

Goblin Whispers

UPSIDE:
Adventure. Childlike trust. Carefree enthusiasm. Optimism. Foolish wisdom. Innocence. Unpredictability. Clarity. Curiosity. Extravagance.

DOWNSIDE:
Aimlessness. Distraction. Carelessness. Mistakes. Recklessness. Caring nothing for others. Pursuing a lonely (if inspired) path.

1: THE CUNNING MAN

The word "cunning" is nowadays most often used to describe someone sly or devious, but in the past it was used to mean both clever and wise. The Cunning Man (or Woman) is an old term that was widely used to describe wizards or magicians (the traditional tarot depiction of this card), whose skill may seem like trickery, but which is actually fuelled by their connection with other worlds.

Magicians, or "cunning men", may be pure faeries or humans with a little faery blood in them, but they are able to see into the hidden realms and can journey there at will. Thus, they are wise people and widely known as healers, practising all kinds of ancient rituals to promote health. As such, they have a lot in common with the shamans of the ancient world, who learned to work with nature — a world that also has a deep connection with Faery.

Here, the Cunning Man plays with apples, assuming the guise of a juggler, an older form of the Magician in traditional tarot. The apples, often known in folklore as being magical, have no power over him, reminding us of his simple, direct wisdom, which has the power to guide us through difficult times.

This card is often associated with the ego. However, it has more to do with an ability to penetrate the outer shell of reality and to delve deeply into the heart of any matter. The Cunning Man seems to invite us to review the deeper reasons behind a problem and see beyond it, passing from a state of uncertainty to its opposite.

The Cunning Man can bring healing through his wisdom, changing destiny and reversing circumstances by engaging with deeper issues. He represents the innate strength of the reader to bring about changes within themselves. On the Downside, however, he can represent a tricky figure with the ability to lead people astray.

Goblin Whispers

UPSIDE:
Skill. Willpower.
Diplomacy. Cleverness.
Trickery. Mind over
matter. Certainty.

DOWNSIDE:
Deceit. Falsehood.
Manipulation.
Chicanery. Illusion.
Indecision. Exploitation.

2: THE ENCHANTRESS

Known as the High Priestess or female Pope in traditional tarot, this striking female figure is here called the Enchantress — due to her faery power to enchant. Wise and powerful, she has a potential to lead astray as well as to guide wisely.

In most early representations, she possesses a great book, to which she may be pointing or turning outward, as if inviting the viewer to read the page she has opened. Here, in the Goblin Market depiction, she is more subtle, hiding her mysteries and making the universal sign of secrecy — placing a finger next to her mouth. Thus, she purveys deeper mysteries — a rich heritage of ancient lore and wisdom, and a penetrating gaze that sees to the heart of all our hopes and desires.

She wears the crescent of the moon on her brow as a sign of her luminous power, while the moon itself may be seen in the sky behind her, drawing its own company of faeries into its sphere of influence.

The Enchantress represents feminine wisdom, the mysteries and a sensitive approach to problems. However, she is by no means a gentle, sweet-natured figure. Her power is of the most profound kind. She is, in some ways, a force that many men flee from, unable to deal with its strength and purity, which far outstrips their own. Her presence often indicates a woman whose advice may be important, but whose influence can, at times, be overwhelming.

Some images show her sitting with her feet on the moon, and it is this moon-powered, intuitive wisdom, shown here in the crescent adorning her head, that governs her influence in the readings where she appears.

Although her wisdom is deep and sensitive, she can also represent an inability to turn wisdom into action; she can lead seekers astray on a path of pride and selfishness; and she may also represent passion out of control, which consumes those who experience it. At her best, however, she is a light that leads the way to greater wisdom.

Goblin Whispers

UPSIDE:
Wisdom. Intuition.
Depth. Teaching.
Willfulness. Modesty.
The sacred feminine.
Fertility of imagination.
The natural world.

DOWNSIDE:
Selfishness. Ignorance.
Self-doubt. Intrigue.
Gossip. False direction.
Secretiveness.

3: The Faery Queen

Although the Faery Queen is not mentioned in the *Goblin Market* poem, she and her consort are found at the heart of all accounts of Faery, making her a key figure in any faery tarot — the equivalent of the Empress in a traditional deck. Here, we see her seated upon her magical throne, surrounded by her goblin courtiers. In her hands she holds the apple of healing and wisdom, and her wings and crowning halo suggest the power of her otherworldliness.

She has many different names. Shakespeare called her Titania, which is thought to come from the name of the Roman goddess Diana. He also called her the faery midwife, who comes to women in labour and delivers their children, but who may steal the newborns away, replacing them with changelings. Proud and wilful, but also glorious and regal, the Faery Queen retains aspects of the goddess Diana. In Welsh faery lore, she is said to be warlike, instructing her courtiers to raid farms for milk, corn and eggs, and cause mayhem wherever they can. The Faery Queen has also been known to send fantastic dreams to haunt sleeping humans.

The Faery Queen embodies many of the *human* qualities of love, particularly the love of a mother for her children. Deeply considerate, her task is to watch over not just her faery courtiers, but anyone who comes to her, whether faery or not — as a protective, nurturing mother would.

In addition, she is the sovereign of romantic love, thus representing a passionate response between couples.

In a reading, she can represent a strong female companion — wife, sister, daughter or friend — whose earthy qualities lend themselves to offering support, but who can be overwhelming. Anyone who has had a destructive experience of a mother's smothering love for her child will recognize the Faery Queen and be wary of her; but for others she is a much-valued companion whose caring nature is both reassuring and enlivening.

The Faery Queen may represent strength of feeling, but, when negatively aspected, can signify too great a reliance on passion and emotion.

Goblin Whispers

UPSIDE:
Passion. Fertility. Health.
The sacred feminine.
Marriage. Wild nature.
Nurture. Protection.
Action.

DOWNSIDE:
Smothering love.
Recklessness. Infidelity.
Inaction. Adultery.

4: THE FAERY KING

The Faery King, depicted traditionally as the Emperor, is said to be the son of the Roman Emperor Julius Caesar and a faery woman called "The Lady of the Secret Isle". Sometimes known as Oberon, he first appeared by name in the medieval French romance *Huon de Bordeaux*, although he is much older in oral faery lore. Like the Faery Queen, the Faery King is best known for his part in Shakespeare's *A Midsummer Night's Dream*.

The Faery King has great powers over nature; he can conjure storms and make rivers flow upstream. If anyone enters his hidden wood, he will speak to them. If they answer, they are said to risk being lost forever, but if they *fail* to answer they are troubled by storms and shrieking voices. Nevertheless, the Faery King is a fount of wisdom, and his passions can stir the soul to great realizations.

Here, he sits upon his golden throne, surrounded by dancing sprites who tend to his every whim. The fruit he holds is a symbol of plenty, while his other hand faces outward, suggesting his power to make us stop and consider.

Above all, the Faery King represents stability. His appearance as the fourth card suggests the "four-square" nature of his power, which he enters into when he sits on his solid, monumental throne.

Like the Faery Queen, the King can be both protective and aggressive; his guardianship, like that of a father, may sometimes seem harsh, but it is most often tempered with love. Nevertheless, his judgement can be summary, so certain is he of his innate power.

In a reading, his presence indicates an authoritative father figure whose words should be weighed up carefully before accepting them. The acceptance of the rules governing society should be tempered with both reason and feeling – something that may be lacking in the Faery King. If a question relates to family, the King may indicate a need to reassess the relationships between fathers and children, although every circumstance will be different.

On the Downside, the King can represent an unstable use of power for its own sake, an overinflated sense of control or a stubbornness that allows little consideration for others.

Goblin Whispers

UPSIDE:
Stability. Authority. Law.
Fatherhood. Solidarity.
Intellect. Conviction.
Forward movement.
Reason. Male authority.
Accomplishment.

DOWNSIDE:
Instability.
Authoritarianism.
Misuse of power.
Tyranny.
Stubbornness.
Immaturity.

5: The Faery Wiseman

The Faery Wiseman – the equivalent of the Hierophant in traditional tarot – is a subtle master of faery magic, with a deep wisdom acknowledged by both faeries and mortals.

Although not always considered a member of the faery race, the Enchanter Merlin from Arthurian legends – an ancient, sage-like being, born of the dark forest and carrying the wisdom of ages – illustrates the kind of knowledge possessed by the Faery Wiseman. Although shown here seated beneath a tree, drawing wisdom from the earth and the sky through the roots and branches of the tree, he may also be encountered walking unfrequented paths through woodland and fields, or leaning on his staff by gates and stiles.

Stories are told of his bright blue gaze, looking deeply into mortal souls and opening the way between head and heart. Some find him forceful and disturbing due to his ability to see into their hopes and desires. Yet he can be generous and kindly, giving advice that is accurate and well-guided. It is said that he has gathered the wisdom of both races – faery and human – and that from them he distils high and low magic. Thus, he is able both to advise and predict the outcome of issues brought before him.

The Faery Wiseman may represent a person (or an inner impulse) that we can turn to for guidance when needed. Yet — in recognition of the trickster aspect of the Faery realm — there is also a sense that we should temper our *belief* in his supreme power with doubt and caution.

Sometimes the Wiseman is seen as a well-meaning but ultimately mistaken teacher, or even a misguided parent, but in faery tradition he is often a deeply magical figure whose wisdom is deferred to even by the faeries.

In readings, this card usually reflects the presence of just such a strong figure, or institution, in one's life — one to whom, or to which, we may turn for help or guidance.

On the Downside, there is a danger that accepting guidance from this person (or from one's inner self) may lead to increased problems, encouraging us to turn away from *other* authority figures. However, the card can also represent valuable personal beliefs that outweigh the more established institutions such as organized religion.

Goblin Whispers

UPSIDE:
High Wisdom. Mercy.
Esoteric knowledge.
Tradition. Inspiration.
Good advice.

DOWNSIDE:
Dogmatism.
Inflexible morality.
Rejection of evident
truths. Instability.

6: THE FAERY LOVERS

Although faery couplings undoubtedly take place, we generally know more of the love affairs between faeries and mortals. In the Welsh tradition, for example the Lady of Llyn Y Fan Fach, who comes from the depths of a magical lake, falls in love with, marries and has children with a local farmer but warns him never to strike her. As so often happens in such stories, promises are broken, and the farmer ends up striking her three times — in each case more playfully than with anger. But on the third strike, the Lady vanishes, taking her magical cattle and her half-mortal children with her. Even in this story, where the ending is unfortunate, Cupid is still present — although perhaps in faery form, more like the faery trickster Puck, who is perhaps best known for leading the lovers astray in Shakespeare's *A Midsummer Night's Dream*.

The associations for the Faery Lovers card stretch all the way from human love to divine love, and everything between, including adolescent love, which is particularly powerful in its ability to overwhelm. The card can represent not only romance and sexual passion but also love of all other aspects of life — family, work, places or the pleasure taken in music, books and art. On another level, it refers to the more remote and transformative love of the divine and the interaction between humans and gods.

The Lovers card has always had a lot to do with choice. Indeed, that is an alternative name for the archetype; love triangles are often depicted. There can therefore be an aspect of uncertainty or instability accompanying its more obvious meanings of love and passion.

In most readings the card serves literally to "marry" – or bring together – the meanings of the cards that surround it. On the Upside, it can represent good communication, while on the Downside, it can represent a lack thereof. People fall in and out of love all the time, and this card may suggest either a burgeoning romance or the end of a relationship.

Goblin Whispers

UPSIDE:
Love. Union. Trust.
Contractual agreement.
Crossroads. Passion.
Impulse. Harmony.
Trials overcome.
Optimism. Choice.

DOWNSIDE:
Separation. Divorce.
Unsettled life.
Reversals. Disharmony.
Uncertainty.
Unwise plans.

7: THE FAERY WAGON

H ere, we see members of the goblin court journeying to the market with their wares — the fruit, flowers, mysteries and secrets that change hands daily in this intriguing place.

The Wagon, or Chariot, in traditional tarot decks is said to balance the Lovers card in that it can represent war — or at least a warrior attitude — in contrast to the gentler energies of love. But there seems to be no such openly warlike nature in the world of the Goblin Market — the only struggle being between the two sisters in the poem: one who accepts all the wonders of Faery and the other who is highly suspicious of them.

The Faery Wagon card is essentially about movement, a journey and/or a struggle to gain momentum. It represents the need to harness both will *and* emotion in order to prevent actions from being impulsive or dangerous; the heart *as well* as the head must rule if one is to obtain one's desired outcomes in life.

Here, we see the Wagon heavily laden, unable to advance without the power of its driver, in this case the Goblin Lord and his cohorts. In readings, this card asks that we allow our ego to be reined in by our emotions, rather than simply advancing with unfeeling, warlike intent.

This card will often appear when there is an issue around fame or fortune, the search for which has overturned many a person. If forethought and emotional balance are brought into play, the outcome of the search can be success and satisfaction; if not, we may well end up falling back down the hill every time we try to climb it.

In every case the inherent meaning of the Faery Wagon is to do with harnessing our best qualities to give us the energy needed for a successful conclusion, whatever that may mean to us. If energies are out of balance, the wheels may literally come off the wagon, leaving the passenger stuck without further movement.

Goblin Whispers

UPSIDE:
Movement. Journey.
Harnessing both will
and emotion.
Trouble overcome.

DOWNSIDE:
Stasis. Failure.
Defeat. Conquest.
Dispute. Bad news.
Over-ambition.

8: The Faery Switch

The Faery Switch is an ancient symbol of faery control used on humans and rebellious goblins. It is portrayed as a branch bearing fruit or leaves, or as a staff, or, here, as a simpler strip of bark.

In the hands of a faery, it can bring complete thraldom of the one at which it is pointed or who is touched by it. The touch of the Faery Switch can bring cessation of movement, transform people into animals or take away their senses. The switch is the probable origin of the magical faery wand, beloved of pantomime tradition. Its power may derive from the yellow chameleon flower, which is said to be planted by faery people and have the capacity to cause changes.

Here, we see the Faery Switch being used to curtail the bad behaviour of a misbehaving goblin; this is how justice (the name for this card in traditional tarot) is meted out in Faery — to bring balance to the seekers who come to the market in search of wisdom and truth.

Faeries are famed for their sense of justice — dishonour them and you will feel the weight of their anger. Here, the powereful faery wears no blindfold, yet they see into the depth of our hearts, requiring us to do the same.

In a reading, this card encourages us to be honest with ourselves and our issues, and act accordingly. It reminds us that if we live with a desire to see the truth, then truth is what we will find; but if we live with a sense of bias, we will remain out of balance. For this reason, the card is crucial, as it offers a just assessment of the situation, to which we should pay the utmost attention.

Where relationships are considered, the Faery Switch indicates a need to be absolutely fair in our dealings. Justice is always impartial and requires us to be the same. If our concern is with our own personal progress, it may indicate a need to reassess our approach and acknowledge that some of our problems may be of our own causing. It also indicates a need to remember that, beyond the *personal* notion, justice is something bigger that we can implement in our dealings with the world.

On the Downside, this card indicates that we may be refusing to see a situation honestly, viewing it from our own selfish point of view. We may blame others for things that we have caused ourselves.

Goblin Whispers

UPSIDE:
Balance. Virtuousness. Justice for all. Harmony. Fairness. Honour. Law. Impartiality. Equilibrium.

DOWNSIDE:
Bias. False witness. Intolerance. Unfairness. Red tape.

9: THE LONE FAERY

The Lone Faery is the equivalent of the Hermit in a traditional tarot deck. A lone faery is a rare thing, since faeries usually tend to congregate in groups. But occasionally one will separate him- or herself from the crowd, as in the case of the Phenoderee, often associated with the Isle of Man. The story goes that he fell in love with a mortal girl, refused to give her up and, as a result, was cast out of the Faery realm, his shape changed into that of a long-nosed, hairy goblin. He chose to live alone after that and became known for his wisdom and helpfulness, often tilling a farmer's field for him, or cooking a meal for a family who had little free time.

Here, the Lone Faery carries the spirit's flame in his lantern, so that he may light the way to a better understanding of life's mysteries. He can thus lead us, if he so desires, more deeply into the world of Faery.

The Lone Faery suggests not only the deep contemplation of events, but also the acknowledgement of the passage of time and the way that this impacts on any issue under consideration. Such acknowledgement allows us to be more detached from the issue, enabling a clearer view of the circumstances that have brought the problem into being.

In a reading, this card can suggest the presence of a teacher or guide who can show ways to reach a point of stillness, enabling us to see what action to take. For this reason, it often also invokes a period of transition; self-awareness, the acknowledgement of the real place we have reached in our journey through life, almost always triggers a change. From the moment the pendulum's swing reaches a point of rest, the only thing that can follow is motion. The card thus suggests movement away from stasis — a triumphant return to a path abandoned, a deepening of awareness of the goals of life.

To reach this we may have to enter into a period of withdrawal, but it is important to keep a finger on the pulse of life in case we become caught in the circle of time and lose our way. When the card appears Downside, this darker side indicates that we may be spending too much time in our own company, becoming isolated from reality.

Goblin Whispers

UPSIDE:
Truth. Time. Honesty. Prudent awareness. Caution. Prophecy. Detachment. Freedom of action. Maturity.

DOWNSIDE:
Isolation. Blindness. Opposition. Imprudence. Immaturity.

10: FORTUNE'S RULE

Even faeries are not exempt from the effects of the Wheel of Fortune, or Fortune's Rule, which may turn at any time and deliver those on its topmost point to the lowest depths.

Faeries have their own effects upon human fortunes, being able to affect them at all kinds of levels, as we see here, where a team of goblins assist the natural procession of time and fate by pushing the wheel so that it turns at their will. Others are carefree enough, safe in their own wisdom and power to lie upon its rim, looking out at the busy world.

The idea of the Wheel of Fortune was dominant in the writings of Medieval and Renaissance philosophers. Everywhere they looked in the world they saw manifestations of this image in the lives and deaths of great men and women, who rose to the top of the wheel and just as rapidly fell as it turned. The Roman goddess of luck, Fortuna, is one of the most powerful deities of the ancient world, ruling over the fortunes of everyone, but in the realm of Faery she seems to have less weight.

What we mean by fortune — whether good or bad — varies enormously according to how we view life. For some, luck is everything — they see events going well or ill and pronounce them to be governed by luck. For others, fortune is something to be worked for, to seek with every ounce of diligence. It may represent something good coming our way, better prospects and greater income; but it can just as easily be the opposite (irrespective of whether the card is Upside or Downside). Fortune can deal us many different hands, and whatever the outcome, we have to deal with it appropriately.

Above all, Fortune's Rule represents change, whether for the better or worse depending on the circumstances. In most readings, the presence of this card can upset the outcome of the messages that the other cards offer — perhaps echoing the tricky nature of our relationship with Faery. Because of this, the normal rules of "Downside" cards, as with reversed cards throughout tarot, are less effective. What appears to represent a negative response or reversal of fortune may turn out to be something else entirely, as only the placing of other cards in the reading will define the true meaning.

Goblin Whispers

UPSIDE:
Destiny. Inevitability of change. Unexpected events. Beginnings and endings. Progress.

DOWNSIDE:
Bad luck. Failure. Reversal of fortunes. Regression.

11: THE SECRET WAY

The more traditional name for the Secret Way card is either Fortitude or Strength. Here, we see a faery willing to explore regions beyond the Faery realm. His strength lies within, and his acknowledgment of the world around him indicates a connection with nature, something shared by most faeries. He does not know where the path will lead, but possesses the strength to traverse it.

Hidden by the hedges that border his lonesome track are the perils of being — to which faeries are just as subject as we are; the fear of "cold iron" is everywhere in the stories of the magical realm because it is created by mankind, and is every bit as dangerous to the faery race as fire or water can be in our own world.

Here the Faery Wanderer (see Card 0) wends his way through a mysterious path, signifying his solitary strength and individuality. This "secret way" is, as we might expect in the magical world, different from that of the physical realm in that it represents strength of feeling, strength of character — even, possibly, moral strength — all of which are present in the worlds where faeries and mortals meet.

The Secret Way represents the strength to keep going even if everything looks hopeless. As such, it has been described as a warrior card, although this risks limiting its power, as strength of will *transcends* the bounds of human ability. Countless tales of heroic achievement — whether warfare, exploration, sport, creativity or beyond — are, however, very much a part of this card's meaning.

In a reading, the Secret Way signifies eagerness and strength of inner resources to attack any problem. It also signifies a need to stop meeting every opposition in a combative way, as strength held in check remains a reserve that you can tap into when needed.

Sometimes we might also need to turn to a powerful friend or guide for support, such as the solitary wanderer we see here, who can help to usher in moments of truth for us to face without fear.

On the Downside, this card can suggest an inability to grasp a problem or to find the energy necessary to combat a difficult situation. Beyond this, it can also be about an inability to master inner fears or to combat the powerful urge to fight our way through any difficult situation.

Goblin Whispers

UPSIDE:
Strength. Force. Courage.
Power. Ability. Authority.
Commanding presence.

DOWNSIDE:
Weakness. Sickness.
Abuse of power.
Indifference. Anger.
Impatience.

12: THE UPSODOWNER

Despite its traditional title of the Hanged Man, there is no indication that the figure is dead. Here, the Upsodowner title suggests a character who can change situations by turning themselves upside-down. The character is simply suspended between heaven and earth — an idea that does not feel out of place given that the card is about turning away from traditional values, sometimes more starkly rendered as treachery.

The Upsodowner hangs by one foot, his head toward the river that waters both the earth and the underworld. But this is no human being — it is a goblin who looks at us with the casual amusement of one secure in his power. So, how did he come to be upside-down? The answer is simple enough. This is someone who turns things upside-down, who swings from the branch with the freedom of one who has *chosen* to be here. He literally turns the world on its head, and, with it, all the meanings of the card in traditional tarot. He is much like the Faery Trickster (see Card 15), but there is a helpful streak in this goblin, as those who encounter him will quickly discover.

As we might guess from the above description, this is a complex card for a number of reasons. It is notoriously ambiguous, and as the figure is already "upside-down", the normal meanings given for upright ("Upside") and reversed ("Downside") cards are sometimes abandoned.

Tarot experts say the card is about getting stuck, literally "hung up" and unable to proceed. The underlying meaning is therefore of a resistance to change of any kind.

Traditionally, the face of the hanged figure tends to be serene, implying that he has mastered his passions and come to terms with life. Here, he is actually *smiling*, challenging us to see the deeper meaning behind the usual interpretation of abrupt and shocking change.

In a reading, the Upsodowner suggests that the best course of action may be to do nothing, and that rather than seeing this as a negative, passive solution, to perceive it as transcending the situation.

The card also indicates a period of transition — a breathing space in which we may learn how to cope with the next stages of our journey.

Goblin Whispers

UPSIDE:
Transition. New insights. Reversals. Acceptance. Change. Rebirth. Sacrifice. Treachery. Intuition. Prophecy.

DOWNSIDE:
Failure to make decisions. Failed promises. Stunted thinking. Being stuck. Egotism. Selfishness. Unjust accusations.

13: THE DARK ONE

In traditional tarot, this is the Death card. But do Faeries have any sense of death? Although long-lived, they do, we believe, reach an end, which seems to be more of a fading than an extinguishing of the spark of life. One might also ask whether faeries are actually alive as we understand ourselves to be? There are simply no final answers to such questions, but the concept of the Dark One captured here, with his scythe, and surrounded by skulls and bones, suggests that there may be an understanding among the faeries of mortality, and thus of the issues surrounding death that affect us humans.

Here, the Dark One raises a finger in admonition, bidding us to remember our humanity. A goblin walks casually along the blade of the scythe, suggesting the faery response to death, and the moon appears over the Dark One's shoulder as a reminder of the changing tides of life.

This is a formidable card. Many readers shy away from its appearance because of the innate fear that we all possess for death. However, death in this instance rarely means physical death, but more often the death of an old idea or way of living, cutting oneself adrift from the stream of things and finding a new way of being. It can also suggest the relief one feels at the end of a protracted struggle — whether with illness or any trenchant problem. Death's scythe is not only used to cut bodies into pieces but also to cut away weeds that strangle new growth.

This card encourages positive change — leaving behind stale, worn-out ways, perhaps changing job, school or relationship — always moving toward a positive outcome. It can also mean disillusionment, an awakening to the recognition that our life needs to change. These are positive aspects of death that can be welcomed as old friends — reflected here by the more lighthearted characteristics of the Dark One, who is portrayed as smiling.

On the Downside, this card can symbolize immobility, stagnation and the inability to accept the need for change.

Goblin Whispers

UPSIDE:
Transformation. Change.
Rebirth. Mortality.
Disillusionment. New
directions. Renewal.

DOWNSIDE:
Stagnation. Inertia.
Discouragement. Failure
to manifest dreams.

14: The Faery Dreamer

The traditional tarot name for this card is Temperance — a concept that, although often associated with refraining from drunkenness, actually has more to do with balance: leading a "temperate" life, with measured responses to issues that occur. The origin of the word temperance is the Latin *temperare*, meaning "to exchange" or "to mingle". Hence the traditional tarot image is of a woman pouring liquid from one vessel to another, representative of the mingling of two streams of energy, or of past and future influences — in order to bring about greater balance. Here, balance is portrayed both in the stance of the faery and in the dancers who skip merrily in the background.

In terms of faery lore, the exchange between the two vessels, as shown on the Goblin Market card here, suggests the ability to move from one realm to another — to be part of the human world while also spending time in Faery. This inevitably connects with the idea of dreams — hence the title of this card; dreams are known to be one of the foremost ways into Faery. In the folk story of Thomas the Rhymer, for example, Thomas dreams of the Faery Queen, only to find himself on awakening by the side of the road along which the faery court is passing.

Goblin Whispers

UPSIDE:
Balance. Patience.
Calmness. Moderation.
Adaptability.
Serenity. Harmony.
Self-control. Mingling
of past and future.

DOWNSIDE:
Discord. Conflict.
Hostility. Frustration.
Competitiveness.
Impatience. Illness.

15: The Faery Trickster

Tricksters are one of the oldest archetypes found in myth and folklore. A being that exists to tease and cause us outrage, and that represents the opposite of the balance created by the Dreamer (see Card 14), the Trickster is associated with devils and demons — the Devil being the trickster's traditional tarot depiction.

But here we are dealing with a Faery Trickster, one of the most encountered beings in the otherworldly realms. He leads strangers astray in marshland, causing them to fall into the mire. This is the beautiful-seeming faery who turns at the last moment into a wolf, its true shape disguised by the power of the trickster hiding.

Recently, the Trickster has become identified with the Greek God Pan, spirit of nature and abandonment, and is often deemed a positive influence rather than an evil one. Despite this, the essential meaning has not changed — the Trickster brings connotations of self-aggrandizement or, if we think in terms of magic, as a magician whose aim is only to raise power for *himself* rather than to help others.

The central meaning of the Faery Trickster revolves around deceit, lies and trickery. The card represents trickster traits being present either in the reader or in someone close to them.

If it represents you, it indicates that you like to break the rules and act selfishly to fulfill your own desires, irrespective of how it affects others. Essentially it is about fear, excessive self-love and the inability to relate to anyone else. Some feel they are too perfect to find anyone who can reach their high standards; others are afraid to acknowledge that anything or anyone matters beyond their own personality. In a more extreme form, this can translate as the feeling that everyone is out to get them.

It is too easy to become trapped in this narrow self-delusion, which will sooner or later lead to the poisoning of life itself. This card suggests a harsh journey that allows individuals to see themselves as they *really* are.

On the Downside, this card has a more positive connotation — suggesting a real effort to free oneself from enslavement to the tricksterish ego.

Goblin Whispers

UPSIDE:
Self-aggrandizement.
Deceit. Power. Passion.
Lack of compassion.
Unprincipled behaviour.
Malevolence. Self-destruction.

DOWNSIDE:
Release from slavery.
Optimism. Concern
for others. Awakening
to the value of the self.
Virtue.

16: THE FALLEN TREE

The road to Faery is often guarded by trees, and you are most likely to encounter faery beings in deep woodlands. So, based on the various references to "leaf-crown'd trees" and "wind-uprooted trees" in Rossetti's poem, we elected to portray the more usual fallen *tower* as a great *tree* here — a tree that, although broken by the lightning strike, is still alive and shaking off the faeries brave enough to have climbed onto its mighty branches.

The traditional tower image is one of the oldest and most consistently reproduced in tarot. Its origins go back to the Middle Ages, where there are references to towers destroyed by lightning and the expulsion of humans from a paradisal realm — a mirror of Faery. Some interpret this card as having destructive and negative aspects; however, there are positive implications, because although the breaking down of old structures and established ways of being may seem frightening, it can ultimately result in positive and powerful restoration and rebirth.

Sometimes we need to face painful, seemingly destructive events in our lives in order for our path to be cleared of old, no-longer-required aspects of our lives (represented by the fallen branches on the card) — and to allow fresh growth.

The immediate response to this card is sometimes one of despair at the thought of disaster and drastic change. However, change is not always a bad thing. The lightning strike might even represent something positive like a flash of insight, inspiration, energy or creativity that will lead to a reassessment of our beliefs, intentions or life path. This reassessment may involve some painful readjustment and difficult confrontation before peace can result.

Few transformations are easy, but if we allow the tree, in whose branches we have established ourselves, to support us, the outcome can be positive and restoring.

On the Downside, the card may mean a failure to recognize the possibility of a *positive* aspect to sudden change. Inevitably, the card's traditional associations with loss and cataclysmic events confront us with shadows of fearful consequences that are hard to move past.

Goblin Whispers

UPSIDE:
Sudden and shocking change. The breaking down of old structures. Clearing the path. Cleansing energy. Reassessment. Catharsis.

DOWNSIDE:
Denial. Failings. Poverty. Unforeseen events. Catastrophe. Loss. Cataclysm. An obstacle to be faced.

17: THE STARRY ROOF

Some of the oldest descriptions of the Faery realm describe it as existing underground. But this is no dark, dank and sinister cavern; rather it is a place of light, often seen as emanating from the stars hidden within the Earth — gems perhaps, or mysterious lights hidden in the roof. Here, the card is called the Starry Roof, rather than the traditional tarot name of the Star.

Many tarot decks show the traditional Star card as a woman pouring water into a stream from two jars, with either five or seven stars in the sky behind her. But here, in the Starry Roof, we see starlight personified as two fairies, jumping for joy, opening their arms and allowing their light to flood out, illuminating everything. The older depiction of the two vessels, representative of the mingling of two streams of energy, is here replaced by two faeries, representing the combined powers of faery and human life.

Essentially, the Starry Roof depicts the rising of hope and positive feelings on a personal horizon. The faery luminescence shows the road ahead, reminding us that we are part of the greater world where stars shed their magical light over everything, painting all in shades of silver, and creating shadows filled with potential meaning.

This card denotes a strong, idealistic approach to events that drives through problems and shines its light into the darkest corners. It is thus a very well-aspected card for times when you are thinking of beginning a new enterprise, moving to a new place or starting over. It has all the vigour and determination that such decisions warrant, and it puts you centre stage like the larger faery depicted here — literally as the star of your own life.

We could think of this card as representing a moment of opportunity — a chance to make the right choice at the right time without fear of mistakes. From the centre of our being, in a place of absolute calm and faery dreaming, we can look out and see with clarity everything that is happening and the possible permutations of any action we take.

On the Downside, the card can suggest that we currently lack the vision to make the right choice, and we should avoid making any irreversible decisions at this time.

Goblin Whispers

UPSIDE:
Hope. Expectation.
Prophecy. Healing.
Rebirth. The gift of light.
Inspiration. Good luck.
Idealism. Destiny.

DOWNSIDE:
Disappointment.
Pessimism. Bad luck.
Stubbornness.
Hopelessness.
Instability.

18: The Moonlit Spell

This card, known as the Moon in traditional tarot, is representative of the way that our satellite casts its spell over everything it touches. Here, the spell is even stronger — made so by the touch of glamorous enchantment provided by the faery as she dances between strange beings made of earth. In essence, she represents the tidal changes that occur during the progress of the moon from new to full and round again, reinforcing the card's association with waxing, waning and cyclicity.

The Moon card may once have been a depiction of the classical lunar Goddesses, Diana and Phoebe, but most decks now tend to show two towers with the moon rising between them, and two dogs or wolves howling at the lunar sphere. Here, the wolves are faery creatures, sending forth their call to enchant us in the spell woven by the faery. Meanwhile the "towers" are mounds of earth with eyes and mouths, which have flame-like faeries dancing atop them, referencing the energy produced by all living things under the influence of the moon.

The oldest meanings for this card tend toward the negative, implying inconsistency and lunar madness. However, for students of faery lore there is a more positive understanding — the moon rules over the tidal energy of human life. As such, the appearance of this card tends to show shifting fortunes — the rise and fall of human affairs.

It also represents synchronicity — the way that seemingly unconnected events come together and influence each other. The ability to see synchronicities often involves a psychic ability, and such abilities should always be treated with caution; otherwise, they can give rise to uncertainty, delusion and even deception. This does not mean that people with psychic gifts should be treated with suspicion; merely that visions need careful consideration.

When we enter the world of Faery, we need the same degree of caution. Balancing the magical with the mundane is important so we do not get caught in a whirlwind of extraordinary events — for ordinary life is also part of Faery.

On the Downside, the Moonlit Spell card can point to a denial of anything "lunar" such as intuitive wisdom, synchronicity and psychic ability.

Goblin Whispers

UPSIDE:
Cyclical challenge.
Dreams. Twilight.
Unconscious urges.
Hidden influences.
Esoteric forces.

DOWNSIDE:
Error. Deception.
Delusion. Madness.
Instability. Fluctuation.
Irrational behaviour.

19: THE SUN ROOM

The radiant light of the Sun pierces everything, with its life-giving rays illuminating even the darkest chambers of the soul. One of the single most unvarying images in the tarot, the Sun card has changed very little over the centuries — representing the constancy of the sun's power, energy and light, which continues all through the year, even in winter when its warmth is obscured.

In many traditional tarot decks either one or two figures are portrayed as playing beneath the rays of the sun; here, in the Sun Room card, we see a whole host of faeries and goblins playing together in the golden light.

The Sun Room is a place of magic and transformation in Irish folklore; the god Aengus mac Oic is said to have kept the beautiful faery Étain there in the shape of a fly; while another otherworldly woman, Aoife, was cast into the form of a crane by Luachra, the wife of the god Mannan mac Lir, and remained there for 200 years. Both these transformations are echoed in the form of the goblin who opens the gates of the Sun Room in this card.

As we would expect from an image so radiant with light, the primary meaning of this card is joy and contentment. It signifies health, wealth and a joyous acceptance of all good things — here, the multitude of delicious fruits exchanged within the Goblin Market.

In a reading, this card suggests happiness and wellbeing, representing the fact that each and every one of us may bring light and pleasure to anyone we encounter — if we so wish. Even in difficult situations the sun's light is always available, enabling us to take a stance of general optimism, bringing light to even the darkest moments, and allowing us to become a warm hub to whom others gravitate.

All the goodness that is present in the card in the upright position can feel as if it has been drained *away* when it appears Downside — turning certainty into uncertainty, triumph into vanity, marriage into divorce, and so on. This might mean that we can't see the light of the sun as a result of the clouds that hang over us — but it's important to remember that the light is still there, behind the clouds.

Goblin Whispers

UPSIDE:
Happiness. Contentment. Joy. Enlightenment. Health. Triumph. Good fortune. Friendship. Marriage. Success.

DOWNSIDE:
Unhappiness. Vanity. Pride. Misunderstanding. Divorce. Discontent. Loneliness.

20: The Queen's Favour

Known as Judgement in traditional tarot, here in the Goblin Market deck, this card is called the Queen's Favour, given that the "judgement" of the Faery Queen, which she willingly gives when asked, is absolute and unchanging. What she says may shift the balance of any previous intention or act.

The Queen's position here — with one hand raised high, finger pointing, and the other low — suggests her ability to understand matters brought to our attention in both the above-ground world inhabited by we humans, and in the below-ground world of the goblins and faeries.

When this card appears in a reading, it generally stands for a call to rise from our current state of being and to prepare for change. In the Faery realm, all seems eternal and unchanging, but, in reality, currents of change are ever-present even there, albeit less clearly observable than in our own world. During the centuries in which we have become aware of the existence of the faery kind, much has changed that has forced them to change also; we are both nearer and further than our closest otherworldly neighbours than at any time before.

Some people will see this card as referring to a judgmental figure or organization that has power over them; others will see it as a need to engage their own inner judge, setting out the pros and cons of the situation in order to decide for themselves on an appropriate action.

In most readings, however, the Queen's Favour suggests a need for change; just how radical will depend on the nature of the issue and the circumstances surrounding it. It can be anything from a simple shift in the way we view a situation to a complete change in the direction of our life.

On the Downside, this card can indicate difficulty in reaching a clearly defined decision and an inability to acknowledge the need for change. It can also suggest that we may be overly self-critical, which can prevent movement of any kind – so do watch out for this in yourself.

Goblin Whispers

UPSIDE:
Judgement. Change. Renewal. Self-assessment. Strong opinions. Outcome. Promotion. Decision.

DOWNSIDE:
Stasis. Postponement. Weakness. Disappointment. Procrastination. Indecision. Delay. Alienation.

21: THE FAERY REALM

Up until now, we have been circling the entrance to the world of Faery — perhaps putting a foot across the threshold, but seldom taking the opportunity to look around and experience the realm of magic and wonder for itself. This, the Faery Realm card, indicates that it is time to go deeper — to explore and get to know the destination that the steps of the Faery Wanderer (in Card 0) have brought us to — the crack between the worlds, the entrance to the cave, the forest, the hidden realm where the Goblin Market offers its riches to us — if only we dare.

The generally accepted meaning of this card, known in traditional tarot as the World, supports this, as it is, in most cases, seen as a reference to completion — to the glorious moments before the world becomes somehow transcendent to us. Here, in the Goblin Market deck, the Faery Queen, who was severe in her role as judge in the previous card, dances in the light of the sun, broadcasting her bounty of fruit, not only to the Faery realm over which she rules, but also to our human world — as a sign of her blessing on those who seek her world with more than just curiosity.

This card is mostly about success — triumph over adversity, and therefore a sense of coming home. Whether the issue has been one of life-changing complexity or a simpler, everyday thing, this card suggests that we have completed our journey and that the outcome is a good one. It implies that we have balanced any conflict that has surrounded us and that we have reached a harmonious place from which we may now review everything that has happened to us along the way. For a person in this position, the way is clear; others will follow us when they perceive our success. Our health is good, our perception sharpened to a point of intensity, and we are the centre around which other things in our life revolve.

On the Downside, the Faery Realm card can represent inertia, stagnation, neglected obligations and plans made coming to nothing — where we may have become mired in a bog of our own creation and be unable to find a way out.

Goblin Whispers

UPSIDE:
Completion. Reward.
Universal truth.
Attainment. Success.
Liberation.

DOWNSIDE:
Inertia. Stagnation.
Loss of vision. Delayed
completion. Failure to
reach a desired goal.

The Minor Arcana

In this section you will get to know the Minor Arcana cards of the Goblin Market deck, which represent subtler levels of meaning within the overall symbolism of the tarot.

You will see that we have used the *traditional* tarot names of Cups and Wands for two of the four suits in this deck, but that we have changed the other two traditional suits (of Coins, or Pentacles; and of Swords) to reflect the faery lore contained in the *Goblin Market* poem that inspired it – by calling them the Suit of Platters and the Suit of Crowns respectively.

Goblin Market Suits	Traditional Tarot Suits
The Suit of Platters	The Suit of Coins, or Pentacles
The Suit of Crowns	The Suit of Swords
The Suit of Cups	The Suit of Cups, or Vessels
The Suit of Wands	The Suit of Wands, or Batons

These symbolic choices will be discussed in the introduction to each of the suits.

In addition, each suit has been assigned a symbolic connection with one of the luscious fruits offered by the goblins in Christina Rossetti's market; plus each suit has a *traditional* ascription to one of the four elements:

Goblin Market Suit	Associated Fruit	Associated Element
The Suit of Platters	Pears	Earth
The Suit of Crowns	Apples	Air
The Suit of Cups	Strawberries	Water
The Suit of Wands	Blackberries	Fire

The folkloric associations of the four fruits (which will be explored in the introduction to each section) add extra flavour to the underlying traditions and meanings of each suit.

You will firstly be given some background information on each suit, including its key themes in the form of evocative "Goblin Whispers". And you will then be guided through the ten pip cards and four court cards of each suit, complete with further "Goblin Whisper" insights into both the "Upside" and "Downside" interpretations.

You will see that the four Goblin Market court cards in each suit have slightly different names than those in traditional tarot.

Goblin Market Court Cards	Traditional Court Cards
Porter	Page
Knight	Knight
Lady	Queen
Lord	King

The Suit of Platters
(traditionally Coins, or Pentacles)

Associated Goblin Market Fruit: Pears
Associated Element: Earth
Goblin Whispers: Finances. Riches. Success.
Caution. Focus. Groundedness.

The Suit of Platters — more commonly called the Suit of Coins, or Pentacles, in traditional tarot — generally represents wealth of one kind or another. Whether shown as coins (a depiction believed to date back to very early times), pentacles (a magical symbol imported in the 19th century), or platters, as here — where we see the richness of the Goblin Market represented by the fruits offered on golden plates to those who visit — this suit represents not just *physical* riches but also the keys to *all-round* success: the wisdom of life and the blessings of house and home. Ruled by the element of earth, it carries the weight and rootedness that holds life together.

In *The Goblin Market Tarot*, the Suit of Platters is associated with pears, the folklore of which is fascinating. Widely distributed around the world and being known of as far away as China, as well as across the whole of Europe, pears are generally seen as bringing good fortune, whatever form that might take.

In classical Greece, pears were numbered among the fruits that were the gifts of the gods; the Roman author Tacitus speaks of runes being carved into pear-tree wood by "the people of the North"; and in ancient Egypt, the pear was sacred to the Goddess Isis — a connection that may be due to the pear tree's great longevity. Throughout Europe the pear is considered as a means of warding off evil. For this reason, pear trees were sometimes planted next to the gate that led to a property — as a defence against unwanted incomers. The Chinese regard it as so sacred that to divide a pear between two people can bring bad luck, and to cut down a pear tree is considered unwise. Pears can also be used in the creation of medicines, especially against toxicity or poisoning. No wonder this fruit is so enthusiastically offered by the goblins!

Ace of Platters

So positive is the influence of the Ace of Platters that it is said to reduce the negative impact of any less favourable ones around it in a reading. Here, we see a goblin offering the gift of a single pear with a smile and an attitude of insouciance. This card suggests great accomplishments, prosperity, good fortune and contentment, although it can also sometimes indicate a tendency to rest on your laurels. Even on the Downside, the card offers visions of wealth and profit — darkened only by a potential emphasis on materialism and the corrupting power of wealth. In other words, if you make it big, just be careful how you let this affect your life.

Goblin Whispers

UPSIDE:
Happiness. Prosperity.
Enchantment.
Accomplishment.
Good fortune.

DOWNSIDE:
Wealth. Materialism.
Corruption. Fool's gold.

Two of Platters

Although the essential meaning of this card is hindrance, blockages, distraction and worry, paradoxically, its interpretation focuses on the success and wealth that can grow out of the fantastic energy of the previous card, the Ace of Platters. This speaks of a simple human problem – that you can be successful, full of bounty and wellbeing, only to then discover that this requires a lot of attention and time to sustain it. As so often in reading the tarot, the answer depends a lot on balancing the energies of more than one card. On the Downside, although successful, you may be caught in a web of ignorance, so keep a careful eye on your finances and other "riches" at this time, as you could easily become a victim of injustice or confusion.

Goblin Whispers

UPSIDE:
Obstacles. Confusion. Entanglement. Agitation. Inconsistent results.

DOWNSIDE:
Ignorance. Injustice. Financial distress. Literary gifts. A letter.

THREE OF PLATTERS

This card represents generous employment — see how the pears on the goblin's platter are offered freely, in the air, with no strings attached. You may be hired to do all kinds of work and gain admiration for the way in which you achieve your aims and work well with others. The spiritual aspect of the card suggests a deepening inner awareness or coming into greater alignment with the faery powers that support you. But in all such matters there is a shadowy side, so that, if the card appears Downside up, you may find yourself unable to carry out the work you have taken on, or spending a lot of your employers' money but producing a substandard product. If, however, you apply yourself honestly to the work, you will almost certainly achieve greatness.

Goblin Whispers

UPSIDE:
Power. Importance. Distinction. Reputation. Success.

DOWNSIDE:
Obscurity. Wastefulness. Extravagance. Laziness. Childishness.

FOUR OF PLATTERS

The traditional interpretations of this card are all about generosity, the giving of gifts to all and the spreading of largesse — the goblin is hastening toward us to share his riches, waving and beckoning in his eagerness. However, the deeper meaning is that you may be showing generosity in order to make others like you; and that, in reality, you may be hanging onto the wealth, only *appearing* to give it away. The Downside of the card implies a feeling of being trapped, as the burden of money weighs you down, potentially halting any progress you are making; and, in the end, the money itself may dry up. However, if you are willing to moderate any growing sense of materialistic delight, you may be able to weather the storm and come out on top.

Goblin Whispers

UPSIDE:
Kindness. Generosity. Gifts. Bonus. Investment. Success in business.

DOWNSIDE:
Delays. Sense of being enclosed. Passing a milestone. Financial problems.

Five of Platters

Originally this whole suit was associated with money — and in the case of this card, lack of it. Most of the more recent tarot experts associate it with loss, destitution and penury, but the earliest accounts suggest it was intended to represent individual effort — the struggle to survive and to desire to create a good life, only implying failure if you didn't manage to *achieve* your goals. The associations with loss of money and/or a turn into more difficult straits, whether at work or elsewhere, can suggest chaos, extending to obsessive feelings becoming soured. Here, we see the goblin racing away, tossing a pear over one shoulder in a casual way — as a reminder to us that gifts given to us can just as easily be taken away, so to stay committed and determined.

Goblin Whispers

UPSIDE:
Struggle. Loss. Toil. Determination. Honesty. Poverty (both physical and spiritual).

DOWNSIDE:
Misconduct. Profligacy. Disorder. Chaos. Troubled love. Obsession.

Six of Platters

This card is about giving gifts to those less well-off than ourselves. Perhaps you have come into a windfall and decide to share it, for example, with deserving friends or a charity of your choice. Alternatively, you may be in the process of deciding who could benefit from your wisdom, or who might succeed you in a role of authority; it isn't always money that is at issue here. Some have seen this as a Robin Hood card, in which the assets acquired may not always have been come by honestly but where there is a desire to pass on the bounty. On the Downside, the card can indicate greed, envy, taking from others and an eagerness to hang onto the money for oneself. We can see from the look on the goblin's face that he is poised to deny us the riches he brings.

Goblin Whispers

UPSIDE:
Gifts. Prosperity.
Philanthropy.
Kindness. The present.
Unexpected events.

DOWNSIDE:
Desire. Greed. Envy.
Jealousy. Avarice.
Ambition.

SEVEN OF PLATTERS

On the one hand, this card is all about gain — money, profit and wealth. On the other, it carries a sense of things getting in the way, slowing down and going nowhere. Older meanings suggest that this has to do with needing to take a break or to purge yourself of the clutter in your life, especially things no longer needed. It can also be a warning not to be too much of a perfectionist. On the Downside, you may find yourself plagued with depression and/or anxiety, which can prevent you from finding a good solution to your issues. But look carefully at your problems, notice the riches the goblin is really offering, then take a deep breath and prepare to weather the storm.

Goblin Whispers

UPSIDE:
Reward for good work.
Money. Wealth.
Profit. Purification.

DOWNSIDE:
Anxiety. Melancholy.
Setbacks. Distrust.
Foolish investments.

Eight of Platters

This card indicates someone who is very practical and organized — someone whose course through life appears smooth, mostly a result of extremely hard work and a highly developed sense of purpose. If this card speaks to you, you are likely to be diligent in whatever you do — whether you're an excellent scholar, a hardworking employee or an employer concerned with the welfare of your workers; if the latter, you are likely to be keen to offer scholarships and take on apprentices. You can, however, have a tendency to be a little "heavy-handed" with people, charging ahead without always thinking before you do. On the Downside, this purposefulness can turn to conceit, concern for others to dishonesty, and intrigue and scholarship to shoddy research. So be sure to watch out for this.

Goblin Whispers

UPSIDE:
Practicality. Scholarship. Purposefulness. Modesty. Equality. Apprenticeship.

DOWNSIDE:
Emptiness. Avarice. Conceit. Insincerity. Intrigue. Dishonesty.

NINE OF PLATTERS

This is a card of fruition — representative of reaching a good and happy conclusion, where all the work you have put in finally pays off. At this point, your life is happy, balanced and productive, as represented here by the goblins all dancing merrily together. Spiritually, the card suggests that you have reached a place of maturity and that your deepest desires are beginning to be fulfilled. On the Downside, the character of the card can display deceitfulness and overindulgence, so be wary of potential theft or swindling, partnerships that could go wrong, and the consequences of your actions, both good and bad.

Goblin Whispers

UPSIDE:
Achievement.
Consequence.
Maturity. Realization.
Contentment.

DOWNSIDE:
Deceit. Guilt.
Disappointment.
Overindulgence.
Swindling.

TEN OF PLATTERS

This card is all about house, home and the balancing of your own small kingdom — just as the goblin here balances the platters bearing the ten pears. It implies that your finances are likely to be secure, and that you might be thinking about leaving a legacy to a child, partner or friend. From the position of head of the house, you can look around you, remembering things that have happened in the past — both victories and defeats. The family line is important to you, so you are aware of the importance of your ancestral lineage. On the Downside, the card can represent chance and gambling — and perhaps losing — all you have gained. You may feel a sense of growing uncertainty as the days tick by that you could lose everything, but be sensitive to the way other cards in the reading may qualify the meaning here.

Goblin Whispers

UPSIDE:
Home. Family. Riches.
Ancestry. Archives.
Legacy. Security. Travel.

DOWNSIDE:
Chance. Hazard.
Destiny. Fate. Loss.
Uncertainty. Insecurity.

PORTER OF PLATTERS

The Goblin Porter of Platters is a perpetual student, fiercely intelligent and devoted to learning. His loyalty to the Faery Queen is absolute, as is his devotion to the work that he undertakes. An excellent negotiator, he or she may be an aspect of you, or one who helps and supports you, offering you the best of the riches in the market. Here, the porter holds out a single pear to you, perhaps a sign of mediation — in order to strengthen your sense of determination toward the issue you are addressing. On the Downside, this card may represent someone who meddles in others' affairs, rather than someone who is trying to help you, so watch out for this.

Goblin Whispers

UPSIDE:
Dedication. Learning.
Apprenticeship.
Trading. Negotiating.

DOWNSIDE:
Meddling.
Overindulgence.
Love of luxury.
Liberal-mindedness.
Bringer of bad news.

Knight of Platters

The Goblin Knight of Platters is a faery prince who is good to have on your side at any time, but especially when you are in a tight spot. His active nature, strength and determination — as indicated here by his readiness to deal with any situation that arises — shows how any situation can be turned around. The card suggests success as a result of determination and knowing how to juggle priorities and work well with others. You are likely to be a careful, obliging type who everyone feels they can depend upon. On the Downside, however, we see a very different character — one so relaxed that you could be perceived as lazy and apathetic, preferring to persuade others to do whatever needs doing rather than do it yourself. In extreme cases, this can affect not only your own dreams but also those of others, so watch out for this.

Goblin Whispers

UPSIDE:
Lucrative action. Success from strength of will. Necessity. Determination.

DOWNSIDE:
Sleepiness. Apathy. Inertia. Stagnation. Idleness. Discouragement.

LADY OF PLATTERS

The Goblin Lady of Platters can be a powerful champion or a difficult partner depending on the circumstances. She is, at times, seen as an aspect of the inner personality that likes to be generous and supportive in all walks of life, whether by throwing an extravagant party or looking after a patient in hospital. As wife and mother, the Lady wants only the best for her partner and children, which can make her over-protective. She can sometimes also be over-generous, here seen tossing away the best fruit from her table for others to enjoy. On the Downside, her good intentions can disappear, only to be replaced by a careless, *laissez-faire* attitude to life. And, at the greatest extreme, she can be vengeful and a sower of discord.

Goblin Whispers

UPSIDE:
Boldness.
Noble-heartedness.
Generosity. Confidence.
Sincerity. Prosperity.
Liberal-mindedness.

DOWNSIDE:
Treachery. Suspicion.
Vacillation. Discord.
Revenge.

LORD OF PLATTERS

The Goblin Lord of Platters is a subtle and intelligent being — someone who has journeyed far and wide, seen both the worlds above and below, and survived many adventures. This has led him to become a settled, wise and nourishing lord. His generosity and creativity — as shown by the abundant platter he holds above his head — reflect the many stages of transformation on offer. His courageous behaviour can act as a magnet, bringing conflicting sides together. His adventurous nature can point the way to many intriguing paths. In a reading, he is a strong and powerful ally who may represent an actual advisor and the inner strength to make wise decisions for yourself, as well as create transformation through your own wisdom. On the Downside, he can be an arrogant and selfish person, who can prevent progress.

Goblin Whispers

UPSIDE:
Creativity. Enterprise.
Generosity. Family.
Adventure. Courage.

DOWNSIDE:
Selfishness. Arrogance.
Suspicion. Antagonism.
Blockages.

The Suit of Crowns
(traditionally Swords)

Associated Goblin Market Fruit: Apples
Associated Element: Air
Goblin Whispers: Ideas. Intellect. Planning. Ambition.
Belief. Sowing of seeds. Sharpness of mind. Struggle.

Concerned with strife and the struggle to grow and change, the Suit of Crowns in this Goblin Market deck replaces the more traditional tarot suit of Swords. Like swords, crowns have long been associated with struggle and conflict, as leaders seek to overwhelm their rivals; and in the world of Faery, we often hear of conflict between rival courts, some of whom respect we humans, while others feel animosity toward us.

Perhaps the fact that the element of air rules this suit suggests that a cleansing breath of wisdom has the capacity to overcome such conflict and darkness. The wisdom of the goblins can help us look at our own struggles and issues until they are clear, and the solutions to them recognizable. In the world of the goblins, crowns represent power and strength in all their forms, and we can see both good and bad uses of such qualities among the cards of this suit.

The apple, long known in faery lore for its magical properties of many kinds, is the fruit associated with the Suit of Crowns. Looking at its associations, we find some remarkable things.

Apples have, in their time, been associated with love, war, temptation and immortality. They have been named as the source of divine inspiration and praised for their healing properties. They are also said to have the capacity to last for as long as two hundred years, and to have thrived as long ago as the Ice Age, with frozen slices of apple having been found in tombs from this period.

In Greek, Roman, Middle Eastern and Celtic mythology, we find all sorts of gods and goddesses linked to apples. In Celtic tradition, for example, Avalon, also known as the Isle of Apples, was ruled over by the Goddess Morgain and her eight sisters, who are believed to guard the sleeping King Arthur to this day. Further North, Norse myths of apples associate them with eternal youth, since their Goddess Idun – the keeper of the orchard and Goddess of the spring – fed the other Norse deities apples to make them immortal. The trickster god Loki then stole the golden ones back in an attempt to make the gods less powerful, but Idun retrieved them and returned their youth and power to the deities.

The most famous lore of apples is perhaps the forbidden fruit of Eden in the Bible, where it represented temptation, while in Classical myth an apple was ultimately the cause of the Trojan War, when Prince Paris awarded one to the goddess Aphrodite, instead of Hera, when he judged their beauty. In Early British tradition, Merlin made a poem to apple trees as he wandered mad in the woods of Caledonia; and, to this day, European farmers bless their apple trees by singing to empower them and keep away evil spirits. Apples, then, seem a fitting fruit to be associated with the Suit of Crowns, given that it represents strength, power and vitality.

In its traditional delineation, this suit would be concerned with swords as meaning "that which cuts away". Here, it is more about creating a boundary to protect us from disorder.

ACE OF CROWNS

The most important aspect of the Ace is the strength it holds. As such, it represents everything that a crown brings with it — purpose, dedication and leadership. However, such power can sometimes overwhelm those who access it. In a reading, this card favours an intellectual response rather than an emotional one. It indicates the need to strip away worn-out ideas and reveal the truth at the heart of the matter. The Ace of Crowns opens up purposeful ways of thinking, encouraging you to look for new ideas or make strategic plans. On the Downside, it can indicate unreasoned anger or even paranoia. So beware of being too ruthless and selfish in your plans or laying down rules and boundaries that risk causing pain to others.

Goblin Whispers

UPSIDE:
Intellect. Overwhelming power. Cutting to the heart of the issue. Initiating ideas and plans. Triumph. Passion.

DOWNSIDE:
Punishment. Excessive commitment. Anger. Embarrassment. Foolish behaviour. Paranoia.

TWO OF CROWNS

Associated with justice, the Two of Crowns is about the quest for balance and harmony — sometimes reconciling two different things in your life and sometimes setting them against each other. If you find yourself feeling pulled in two directions at once, you may need to struggle to find the fulcrum of harmony, but the resulting effort will reward you with greater clarity and certainty. On the Upside, this card could mean that you can draw support from a stable source, such as a close friend or ally. However, on the Downside, you might find yourself facing deception and duplicity. Watch out, therefore, for people seeking to unbalance matters rather than help you toward positive solutions.

Goblin Whispers

UPSIDE:
Balance. Harmony.
Friendship.
Attachment.

DOWNSIDE:
Falseness. Duplicity.
Misrepresentation.
Dishonour. Lies.

THREE OF CROWNS

A card of disharmony, sorrowful events, sadness and breaking apart, people can often find the presence of the Three of Crowns difficult to take in a reading, as it tends to point to a threatened breakdown, the end of a relationship, or events conspiring to move you away from a point of rest into a maelstrom of harsh water. Fortunately, other cards in your reading can dissipate the sense of doom and gloom, reminding you to work through this period with a sense of trust that love and courage will help you to re-establish a more balanced state of being. On the Downside, the emphasis of this card is on the darker aspects of life, such as confusion, loneliness and feelings of alienation. Are the two goblins on either side of the central figure jailers or supporters?

Goblin Whispers

UPSIDE:
Sorrow. Departure.
Separation. Aversion.
Unrequited love.
Loss. Tears.

DOWNSIDE:
Alienation. Loneliness.
Madness. Confusion.
Misjudgement. Warfare.

Four of Crowns

After the woes of the Three of Crowns, the Four of Crowns offers a respite. Following storms and upsets, here, the seeker withdraws to live a hermit-like existence for a time — in which it is possible to live frugally, to take stock of loss, and to prepare to re-emerge enlivened into the world. There is, however, also a sense in this of being banished and of having to leave old ways in order to enter into new. Perhaps we can see this in the stance of the goblin here, who sits alone, as if suspended between two worlds. On the Downside, this card suggests that through considered action we may learn and gain strength from any sense of loss or abandonment. Advice from a doctor or spiritual advisor may also be indicated by this card.

Goblin Whispers

UPSIDE:
Solitude. Respite.
Exile. Banishment.
Abandonment.
Withdrawal. Recovery.

DOWNSIDE:
Wise economy.
Prudence. Harmony.
Music.

FIVE OF CROWNS

The Five of Crowns tends to be about abandonment and betrayal. It is virtually impossible to escape its negative aspects, since it means pretty much the same thing whether it appears Upside or Downside in a reading. It can, however, be affected by the cards that attend it, reminding us that we must sometimes accept some inevitable difficulties in order to transcend a situation. Depending on the nature of the reading, you may be feeling abandoned or neglected. However, there is still a chance to move beyond the immediate situation if you can succeed in getting your inner prejudices out of the way, or, even more importantly, if you can learn how to ask for help.

Goblin Whispers

UPSIDE:
Anxiety. Loss. Misfortune. Setback. Humiliation.

DOWNSIDE:
Grief. Defeat. Loss. Trouble.

Six of Crowns

The casual insouciance of the goblin in this Six of Crowns card fits well with its essential meaning, which is all about journeys. There are so many reasons that we might undertake a journey. It may be to another country, to a new place of work or to a new idea, or it can even refer to the journey of the spirit beyond life. The most important theme of this card is, however, a movement from stale or worn-out ideas or situations, toward a more satisfactory place or state of mind. On the Downside, the card may represent finding yourself in a backwater from which it is hard to escape. When this is the case, to try to move at all may cause greater problems, which means that it is sometimes best simply to wait out the situation until things improve.

Goblin Whispers

UPSIDE:
Journey. Travel.
Holiday. Messenger.
Moving away for safety.

DOWNSIDE:
Immobility. Revelation.
Surprise. Feeling lost.

SEVEN OF CROWNS

This card is all about finding hope in the most dire circumstances. After the succession of difficult cards in this suit — from three to six — it comes as something of a relief, as we may see from the smile of freedom on the face of the goblin here, as he spreads his wings to fly. But all is not as clear as it may at first seem. While you may be able to approach problems with a clear, positive outlook, on the Downside this card implies new problems that might come along — whether slander, news of danger ahead or whatever else. The overall message, however, is optimistic: that if you believe in yourself and advance with caution, then, with a little help, you have a good chance of achieving your dreams, however great they are.

Goblin Whispers

UPSIDE:
Hope. New plans.
Perseverance.
Self-belief. Realization
of dreams.

DOWNSIDE:
Advice. Instruction.
Warning. Slander.

Eight of Crowns

In this card we see a crown-carrying goblin balletically leaping into the air to prevent being caught and held by the goblin below. As such, it is all about avoiding anything that prevents you from moving forward. In a work situation, for example, tasks may be delayed or affected by criticism or condemnation by a superior. Healthwise, it might suggest an illness that could keep you at home. Yet, interestingly, on closer consideration, it will often prove to be just *you* holding *yourself* back, which means that, if you can weather the storm, you will find a way forward. On the Downside, this card is a reminder that we should be careful of cutting any bonds that hold us too suddenly, as we may not have the strength to maintain our balance.

Goblin Whispers

UPSIDE:
Criticism. Crisis.
Blame. Censure.
Condemnation. Illness.
Restitution.

DOWNSIDE:
Delay. Obstacles.
Accident. Misfortune.
Mistaken perceptions.

Nine of Crowns

This card is often taken to mean that a difficult choice lies ahead — one that may lead to sacrifice or loss. It can also suggest a timid person who is the victim of slander or gossip and who lacks the strength to defend him- or herself. This might be referring to someone who is close to you, rather than you; thus, you are likely to be afflicted by anxiety within yourself for the other person. The goblin here shows his concern and raises his hands to invoke peace. On the Downside, the term "reasonable fear" leaps out, suggesting that you check in with yourself to see if you have every *reason* to feel this emotion or if it may be unfounded. It's always important to look for balance at such times.

Goblin Whispers

UPSIDE:
Anxiety. Worry.
Despair. Suffering.
Isolation. Envy. Loss.

DOWNSIDE:
Doubt. Suspicion.
Reasonable fear.
Timidity. Disgrace.

TEN OF CROWNS

Considered one of the most difficult cards in the deck, the Ten of Crowns seems to point to disaster and disappointment. Whatever the issue you are concerned with, there could be misfortune or sadness involved. Fortunately, the grimmer aspects of the card can often be mitigated by the other cards in a reading, hence the card showing the central goblin being supported by nine others. One interpretation is that this card suggests the end of a relationship that has been destructive even if this sense of destruction has not been recognized until now. Any sense of pain or ruin can be seen as a means toward freedom and new beginnings. On the Downside, the card can indicate potential signs of improvement in your situation, although these are likely to be short-lived.

Goblin Whispers

UPSIDE:
Pain. Ruin. Sadness.
Desolation. Tears.
Misfortune. Exhaustion.
Disappointment.

DOWNSIDE:
Temporary benefit.
Improvement.
Short-lived success.

PORTER OF CROWNS

What is the Goblin Porter thinking? What do his actions mean? This card often represents someone who is quick to offer advice or comment on a situation, not always with any real information. He, or she, loves the attention of the crowd and will tend to rush in without thinking, or advise you to do the same. You may be dazzled by his starry nature; but be careful lest his light shows too much. On the Downside, the Goblin Porter is often at a loss for words but tries to compensate for this by embroidering the truth. Because of this he can exaggerate problems by putting on an act.

Goblin Whispers

UPSIDE:
Impulsiveness.
Curiosity. Insight.
Vigilance. Agility.

DOWNSIDE:
Superficiality.
Lack of preparation.
Powerlessness.
Weakness.
An imposter.

KNIGHT OF CROWNS

The Goblin Knight is a good person to have on your side in a tight spot as he can be ruthless and tends not to acknowledge boundaries, preferring to charge on regardless of others. While his strength is great, it is often accompanied by a lack of discipline that can make him seem wild and out of control. However, there is also a certain sense of innocence about him. In a reading, this card suggests that any of these qualities may be present either in the issue that you are concerned with or in your own actions. So be careful not to get too carried away in your eagerness to win. On the Downside, the Goblin Knight can become careless as well as carefree, making him a risky companion. There are times in life when you could do with a more restrained character to guide you, or a less aggressive aspect of your own character to rule the situation.

Goblin Whispers

UPSIDE:
Bravery. Skill. Strength.
Heroic action.
Championing a cause.

DOWNSIDE:
Imprudence. Conceit.
Impulsive actions.
Restrictive rules.

LADY OF CROWNS

Here, we see the Goblin Lady of Crowns hold court from mid-air, surrounded by her goblin servants. Although she can, at times, be a stern judge and a fierce critic, her wisdom shines through everything she says and does and, as such, she is a shrewd and perceptive ally on the journey through life. Her presence in a reading calls us to take stock of where we are and what we truly desire; whatever question we *think* we have asked, there may be a deeper issue beneath the more superficial question. On the Downside, the Goblin Lady of Crowns can tend to be overly critical and can also radiate secret sorrow.

Goblin Whispers

UPSIDE:
Maturity. Insight. Perception. Visionary gifts. Subtlety. Quickness. Accuracy. Grace. Wisdom.

DOWNSIDE:
Sorrow. Loneliness. Misjudgment. Being over-critical.

Lord of Crowns

Traditionally described as an advisor, a powerful supporter and a guide, the Lord of Crowns represents discipline, firmness and a dedication to duty that must be acknowledged. He may also represent a judge, someone of high rank in a business organization, a senior churchman or a commander in the armed forces. As such, he is a person whose authority is seldom challenged, although this does not, of course, mean that he is always right. In the context of this suit, his influence is strong, as we may judge by his self-satisfied smile. On the Downside, he represents a domineering figure whose cruelty and lack of sympathy toward those around him can make him more likely to cause conflict than prevent it.

Goblin Whispers

UPSIDE:
Power. Command.
Force. Intelligence.
Priest. Judge. Counsellor.
Businessman.

DOWNSIDE:
Despot. Enemy. Cruelty.
Conflict. Evil intent.

The Suit of Cups

Traditionally, the Suit of Cups — characterized by imagery of vessels, both sacred and mundane, and the liquid they contain — is all about the emotions, revealing both how *we* feel and how others may feel about us; the image of flowing water has been associated with the emotions since ancient times.

The symbolic cup imagery of this suit may make us think of the Holy Grail — that most famous symbol of light, life and transformation — or the cauldrons of inspiration beloved of the Celts. Here, in *The Goblin Market Tarot*, we have sought to portray a more basic container, full of wine and ale as well as spiritual sustenance. And since these are *faery* cups, they are also filled with enchantment, light and wisdom. So drink heartily, friends!

The fruit favoured by the goblins for this suit is strawberries — a plant long associated with feminine magic and fertility. Goddesses such as Venus, Aphrodite,

Freyja and even the Virgin Mary have been linked to the strawberry, which has long been held to be helpful in both healing and matters of love. In Bavaria, to hang a cluster of strawberries from the horns of a cow is believed to ensure a good milk yield by acting as a gift to the spirits or faeries in exchange for blessing the cow. In various traditions, it is believed that if a pregnant woman carries strawberry leaves in her pocket, it can help with labour pains. The ancient Romans also loved strawberries, distilling them to treat various digestive complaints, while in ancient China the Emperor made tea from strawberry leaves as an antidote to ageing. All in all, the strawberry is a magical fruit loved by the goblins as much as it is by most humans.

Ace of Cups

The faery holding the cup here shines with her own inner light and presents the vessel to us as her greatest gift, lifting her forefinger in an ancient sign of blessing. When translated into the life of an individual deck user, the spirituality and emotional foundation of this card becomes indicative of home life, family, fertility and generosity of spirit; the person represented here is a fount of love, wisdom and good spirit. He or she loves to bring good news and to offer every kind of nourishment to those around them. This is also a card of good omens, suggesting that any new enterprise will flourish and grow. On the Downside, the implication of the card is of change, a sense of loss and a sterility that can push you back on yourself, leaving you feeling stuck in the past.

Goblin Whispers

UPSIDE:
Home. Family. Fertility.
Feast. Nourishment.
Good cheer. Good news.
Transcendence. Love.

DOWNSIDE:
Change. Unrequited
love. Metamorphosis.
Inconstancy. Sterility.

TWO OF CUPS

The meaning of this card is simple — it is about love, harmony, closeness, attraction and partnership. The goblin here is in a hurry to offer the cups of plenty that he carries to those who deserve them. If marriage is contemplated, it is likely to be a good one; and relationship problems of any kind can be mitigated by the energy of this card. The aspect of choice is also present here, suggested by the two streams of water flowing together beneath him, as is also depicted in traditional tarot. On the Downside, whether in personal relationships or work ones, this card suggests disharmony, a breakdown in understanding and communication, a quarrelsome relationship in which people who were once close are now divided, and even, at extremes, divorce.

Goblin Whispers

UPSIDE:

Relationships. Empathy.
Friendship. Attraction.
Passion. Kindness. Love.
Marriage. Partnership.

DOWNSIDE:

Envy. Greed. Lust.
Opposition. Longing.
Quarrel. Conflict.
Infidelity.

THREE OF CUPS

The goblins here are raising a magical cup in acknowledgement of the deck user. This fits well with the meaning of this card, which is to do with celebrating success, supporting vision and inspiring people to greater heights. It also encourages pleasure, enjoyment and mirth, and if you have been sick, it points the way to recovery and healing. On the Downside, this card is less cheerful, as it suggests that you may find yourself spending a lot of time on your own, feeling unhappy, with a sense of jealousy about the success of others, or joining with others who feel envious. Blockages and even the suggestion of overindulgence is all part of this. Be wary of addictions or accidents, as well as those who might seek to puncture the bubble of your success.

Goblin Whispers

UPSIDE:
Celebration. Perfection. Success. Renown. Relief. Fruitfulness. Recovery. Pregnancy. Healing.

DOWNSIDE:
Setback. Termination. Accidents. Obstacles. Overindulgence.

FOUR OF CUPS

The interpretation of this card can stretch all the way from dullness through extreme boredom to, at times, self-loathing; the curious goblins gather around a central flame here but seem unable to engage with it. Representative of feeling divided, stressed and weary after too much work, this card can be seen as an invitation to a period of rest and reflection, where you try to believe in yourself and avoid harbouring bitterness toward others. On the Downside, the meaning is more pleasant, encouraging you to look for new directions in life and for unexpected gifts that will transform your journey. However, be sensitive to your physical needs, with an awareness that you may feel tired at times.

Goblin Whispers

UPSIDE:
Weariness.
Dejection. Boredom.
Dissatisfaction.
Affliction. Bitterness.
Being stuck.

DOWNSIDE:
Novelty. New knowledge. A sign.
Premonition.
Foreboding.

FIVE OF CUPS

There is little to enjoy about this card in its upright position, although you'll see that for once the Downside outcome is more positive. The Upside meaning focuses on despair, loss and ignorance — although this rather bleak interpretation can encourage you to look for a significant turning point in your life — a moment when the correct decision may mean everything. On the Downside, the card offers hope, alliances with friends or family and, above all, illumination, which breaks through the dark clouds and lets in the truth. The card invites you to heal old wounds that may have divided you from the rest of your family.

Goblin Whispers

UPSIDE:
Suffering. Grief. Loss. Disempowerment. Regret. Deceit.

DOWNSIDE:
Hope. Alliance. Family reunion. Ancestors.

Six of Cups

Essentially, this card, often depicted as an adult looking back to childhood, is about nostalgia. Here, the goblin dances with child-like glee, tossing away his lucky apple and spilling his cups. This may serve to remind us that the act of turning to the past can sometimes show us things that are disturbing or shocking – things that we think we remember in one way can turn out to be very different in reality. On the Downside, the card encourages us to look forward, seeing the way ahead as it really is, making this card better aspected when read in this reversed position than in its upright position.

Goblin Whispers

UPSIDE:
Looking backward. Forgotten pasts. Uncertain outcomes. Inheritance. Ancient quarrels stirred up again. Strife. Vanity.

DOWNSIDE:
Looking ahead. Memories. Gifts. Old friendships restored.

SEVEN OF CUPS

This is a card for dreamers — those who fashion wonderful castles from clouds that may all too soon melt way. It reminds you to be careful not to become too enraptured by your own plans, nor too delighted by your own thoughts — as symbolized here by the goblin tossing aside her cups in a blaze of excitement. If you are essentially a follower rather than a leader, it's a sign to be careful of being led astray on paths of moonlight; the plans of others may seem perfect, while they are, in fact, hollow. On the Downside, this card represents a stronger will and determination. However, this could end up serving only to strengthen your dependency on the vision you have built. So try to look clearly at things to see the truth of the situation, as the desire to achieve success, or to win in love, may confuse the real issues here.

Goblin Whispers

UPSIDE:
Plans. Flights of fancy.
Illusion of success.
Over-imagination.

DOWNSIDE:
False plans. Aspirations.
Desire. Willpower.
Determination.

EIGHT OF CUPS

Whether you are undertaking a new role in the workplace, or a new relationship, this card means that you could find yourself plagued by uncertainty. A sense of disappointment may overwhelm you, and if you feel drawn to follow a certain path, feelings of timidity may cause you to pause; the goblin here looks into the cup but sees only his reflection looking back. Yet, the Eight of Cups is also one of the so-called travel cards, with the journey here likely to be a spiritual one. On the Downside, the card implies a return to health and vigour after an illness. Getting to know old friends and reconnecting with family members you may have lost touch with is also present, but be careful of the desire to spend too much time with others, leaving you with no time for yourself.

Goblin Whispers

UPSIDE:
Attachment. Timidity. Doubt. Fear. Disappointment.

DOWNSIDE:
Happiness. Satisfaction. Family. Apology. Debts paid.

NINE OF CUPS

The Nine of Cups represents a successful outcome, a renewal of energy and the gift of problem-solving; the goblin floats above the water with evident delight. Yet this exuberance may be tempered by a sense of excessive indulgence in pleasure or winning for its own sake, which can unbalance us if we are not careful. Material success may be offered but end up making us feel isolated. On the Downside, we find these aspects even more powerfully represented, with errors and imperfections sometimes affecting the positive aspects of honesty, loyalty and freedom. You may, as a result, find that speaking your mind ends up getting you in worse trouble than keeping silent.

Goblin Whispers

UPSIDE:
Victory. Success. Triumph. Delighting in pleasure. Problems solved.

DOWNSIDE:
Error. Imperfection. Honesty. Loyalty. Candour. Affluence.

TEN OF CUPS

This card represents a sense of home and emotional security – a desire to rush home from the Goblin Market to your city, town or village, which you see as the centre of your universe, and to those who dwell there, who you see as your tribe.

The fact that your dreams are homed here can create waves of delight, passion and contentment. But you should be careful of becoming overwhelmed or having your ego inflated. Here, the goblin hovers alone above a central cup, looking out at the mouths of the other nine cups, representing family, love and contentment. On the Downside, we may not be able to see the submerged cups, as the sun goes behind a cloud, making our perfect world look less attractive. Quarrels with family members or partners can become frequent events, and you could find yourself engaged in physical conflict with someone who has upset you.

Goblin Whispers

UPSIDE:
Home. Welfare.
Contentment. Security.
People close to you.

DOWNSIDE:
Anger. Indignation.
Insult. Irritation.
Quarrels.

PORTER OF CUPS

The Goblin Porter of Cups is a shining star of loyalty, devotion and application. As a guide, he gives himself wholeheartedly to study and learning. Here, he seems to be challenging us to take the cup, or the proffered strawberry.

If you are a student, this card is likely to signify that you have the ability to apply yourself to everything you do; if not, you are likely to be in love with knowledge. This card also represents discretion, suggesting that you are the ideal person to whom secrets may be safely told. On the Downside, the character of the Goblin Porter becomes weak and vacillating, given over to envy at the achievements of others, and perhaps seeking to seduce those who can help further one's own course through life. He can also be cunning in his behaviour.

Goblin Whispers

UPSIDE:
Loyalty. Devotion.
Studiousness. Work.
Learning. Reflection.
Discretion.

DOWNSIDE:
Weak will. Heartache.
Envy. Jealousy. Flattery.
Seduction.

KNIGHT OF CUPS

The Goblin Knight of Cups is a person of perfect gentleness and spiritual daring. In the realm of Faery, he would be destined to be the cupbearer to the Faery Queen herself — a position of great esteem. In the ordinary world, he is an idealistic dreamer whose charms most people find hard to resist. A sense of otherworldly glamour and intrigue hangs about him — as if he has a secret knowledge hidden just below the surface. As a guide he is second to none, and as a friend he is a rock upon which you may rest in times of need. On the Downside, however, his character can become deceitful and seductive — a cheat and a trickster who could lead you astray or encourage you to do what you should not.

Goblin Whispers

UPSIDE:
Invitation. Proposal. Attraction. Compliance. Arrival. Conquest. Union.

DOWNSIDE:
Guile. Seduction. Fraud. Cunning. Deception. Trickster.

LADY OF CUPS

The Goblin Lady of Cups is something of a visionary and prophetess, as well as a good friend and confidant. She is also a truth speaker, which can, at times, make her a difficult ally. However, her compassion and honesty make her someone to whom we can turn in times of crisis. Empathic and supportive, we see her dancing here within the cup of emotional gratification, drawing on the energies of both the moon and a star to encourage the freedom to allow *all* emotions full rein in the search for truth. On the Downside, she might lead you astray with emotional twists and turns, so be careful of any false glamour or unclear guidance on her part.

Goblin Whispers

UPSIDE:
Honesty. Loyalty.
Devotion. Wisdom.
Truth. Balance.
Emotional expression.
Humanity.

DOWNSIDE:
Untrustworthiness.
Dishonour. Corruption.
False guidance.
Emotional ambivalence.

Lord of Cups

The Goblin Lord of Cups is generous, talented, compassionate and overflowing with confidence. He might be a figure in your life such as an artist, a banker, a priest or a doctor in whom you place much trust. At a basic level, he represents the kind of person who inspires others, offering sympathy and generosity to all, and if at the head of a family, he will always offer nurture and care. However, he can, at times, be unwilling or unable to share emotional bonds; here, the goblin is seen raising his cup to a cheering crowd, but his glance is somewhat unfocused and his eye wanders. On the Downside, he can become a weak and vacillating friend and an unstable partner (whether in business or in love) who is easily diverted onto different paths, and who can be prone to self-pity.

Goblin Whispers

UPSIDE:
Honesty. Integrity. Kindness. Equality. A scientist. An artist.

DOWNSIDE:
Dishonesty. Double-dealing. Extortion. Corruption.

The Suit of Wands

Associated Goblin Market Fruit: Blackberries
Associated Element: Fire
Goblin Whispers: Enterprise. Determination.
Passion. Energy. Impulsiveness. Volatility.

As one might expect, the Wands of this suit are faery wands, and as such may be tricky and liable to turn traditional tarot meanings for this suite on their heads.

The Goblin Market fruit associated with this suit is the blackberry — a plant that has a chequered career in folklore. Berries are said to be symbolic of all sorts, from representing the blood of the gods to being signs of impending death; and the blackberry — with its reddish tinge that gradually turns black — has many more stringent associations. Folklore tells us that its colour is because of Lucifer, the fallen angel, landing in a blackberry bush when he was thrown out of heaven — turning what had previously been a red bush to black with his spittle. Older myths involve blackberries as a form of punishment for mortals who try to steal from the gods. Thus, for example, the character Bellerophon, in Greek mythology, being thrown off the winged horse Pegasus when attempting to ride it to Mount Olympus (home of the gods), and being blinded by the thorns in a blackberry bush, when he landed in it. Another folk tale from Middle Europe describes a man jumping into a bush in his eagerness to get to the fruit and likewise losing his sight, but then being able to regain it by jumping backward out of the bush. We can see, then, that the blackberry clearly has a tricky and potentially dangerous side, making it a perfect companion to the sometimes spiteful nature of the goblin race.

Although wands can be made from most types of wood, the connection with *blackberry* in the Goblin Market deck is a reminder to be wary, given that the spikey nature of the blackberry bush can catch in either clothing or flesh when one walks by it.

Look carefully at how the faery beings wield their wands in this suit, never forgetting that they are filled with power subject to many different kinds of use. Some may be used for help, others to hinder. The faery beings, especially the goblins, like to play tricks on us and may lead us to trouble as well as success.

ACE OF WANDS

This is a great card of beginnings. It suggests a "go-forward" state in which you can hardly fail in whatever enterprise you are attempting, or whatever issue you are facing. It encourages you to take action, to move forward with confidence — hence the intent expression on the face of the faery chief holding his wand with its powerful Sidhe symbol (see page 22). The card is often associated with birth — either of an idea or of an actual child. On the Downside, the card indicates that you should think twice before you proceed. Such words as "ruin", "defeat" and "collapse" are often invoked by this reversed card, so be aware that any new enterprise could run into rough waters.

Goblin Whispers

UPSIDE:
Birth. Beginning.
Creativity. Invention.
Enterprise.
Empowerment.

DOWNSIDE:
Ending. Downfall.
Bankruptcy. Decline.
Persecution. Collapse.

TWO OF WANDS

D espite the negative interpretations of melancholy, anger and darkness often placed on this card, it can stand for new possibilities. It is often said to represent a quarrelsome, angry person who tends to clash with those in authority. But it may also be someone who is in a position of great power, who has reached the pinnacle of their life and yet finds no satisfaction. It can represent the closeness of friends, as the two goblins here show us. One of the Downsides is a sense of enchantment, which might sometimes hide the sight of a path leading away from the burden of too much success to a place where there is space for new possibilities to be recognized.

Goblin Whispers

UPSIDE:
Achievements. Dark thoughts. Dominance. Hot temper. Boldness. Determination. Maturity. Quarrels. New possibilities.

DOWNSIDE:
Surprise. Melancholy. Anger. Despair. Fear. Loss of possessions. Fresh starts.

THREE OF WANDS

This card represents action, movement into a new dimension of activity and/or a voyage of discovery into fresh waters. It is a sign to be bold and courageous in your activities, to expect success as you move forward, and to look for those who will support you, share your vision and co-operate with you at every level, as the guardian goblin does for his friends on this card. Just as you're likely to feel energized by the sun's rays in an Upside reading, when the card appears Downside, you may feel disempowered, so that setting a new project or long-held dream in motion may seem like too much of a struggle.

Goblin Whispers

UPSIDE:
Enterprise. Trade.
Activity. Boldness.
Courage. Voyages
of discovery.
Co-operation.

DOWNSIDE:
Struggle. Loss of energy.
Feeling defeated.

Four of Wands

One of the few cards that demonstrates virtually the same meaning whether Upside or Downside, the Four of Wands indicates coming home to a joyful welcome. It is all about the unity of a stable society, whether represented by family members, a group of friends, co-workers or a country. It suggests that it is a good idea to re-establish any old alliances that have fallen by the wayside, and in general to acknowledge the value of friends, family and ancestors, as well as the value of tried and tested ideas. In other words, it suggests a balancing act, as displayed by the goblin's display of balance above the flames of truth here. The Downside aspect of the card, although still generally positive, indicates that you may not be fully acknowledging those who have helped you along the way on your journey through life.

Goblin Whispers

UPSIDE:
Homecoming. Mirth.
Community. Alliance.
Reunion. Beauty.

DOWNSIDE:
Prosperity. Advancement.
Failure to acknowledge
help. Loss of direction.

FIVE OF WANDS

The main thrust of this card's meaning is wealth and abundance in every aspect of life. Although it is therefore well-aspected, there is an inherent danger that overconfidence or excessive pride could lead to a breakdown in communication and a lesser degree of success. Too often when everything is handed to us on a silver plate, we forget that riches carry their own *shadow* aspect. For example, while wealth may provide a form of power on the surface, it can also hide a multitude of weaknesses. When this card appears Downside, indicating dispute, litigation or conflict, a degree of weakness can become clear. The conflict suggested by this is evident in the way the two goblins at the centre of the card seem to be struggling against each other.

Goblin Whispers

UPSIDE:
Success. Abundance.
Overweening pride.
Rivalry. Luxury.

DOWNSIDE:
Conflict. Dispute.
Contention. Challenge.
Turn-about.

Six of Wands

This is a card for those who keep the home, who care for the family and who tend to all things domestic in order to maintain an even keel. It can also suggest the imminent arrival of someone with a message of hope or goodwill, such as is potentially being delivered through the action of the wand carried by the goblin here. This card may suggest you finding yourself revered and placed in a position of increasing strength and reliance – if you are, for example, a good team leader, with all the stress that this entails. On the Downside, however, it suggests a need to be wary of unnecessary delays, jealousy or betrayal, whether at work or at home. As in most readings, the meanings may be mitigated by surrounding cards.

Goblin Whispers

UPSIDE:
Family life.
Housekeeping.
Good-news messages.
Progress. Triumph.

DOWNSIDE:
Infidelity. Treachery.
Disloyalty. Betrayal.
Delays. Bad service.

Seven of Wands

This card is about a successful outcome after prolonged struggle. You have ascended the tower, climbed the hill or scaled the mountain, and, now at the top, you can look around and see all that is yours to command. The goblin here hastens under the light of the sun to bring you good news, like a runner in a relay race. The pendulum has swung high for you so now is the time to take stock, to measure the extent of your ambition and to begin to set in motion all that is necessary to implement your future goals. On the Downside, this card can suggest indecision — to the extent that you may be unable to find a way forward. Sometimes this is the result of feeling victimized, or simply of anxiety and self-doubt.

Goblin Whispers

UPSIDE:
Success. Advantage over others. Profit. Goal attainment. The need to take stock.

DOWNSIDE:
Anxiety. Embarrassment. Indecision. Doubt.

Eight of Wands

After the struggle to succeed in the Seven of Wands comes the respite of this card — the satisfaction of a job well done, with time to rest and reflect. This card traditionally speaks of going to the countryside for refreshment. Some suggest that it may also be about falling in love, and this works well with the idea of taking time to rest and review the direction of your life. During such times, we often have time to notice the people who are most special to us, the ones who reflect our vision back to us, like the mirrored goblin on this card. The card can also signify events moving quickly and contracts being completed, perhaps in the purchase of a house, for example. On the Downside, you may find yourself plagued by disputes, jealousy and a feeling of regret for opportunities lost.

Goblin Whispers

UPSIDE:
Appreciation. Progress.
Completion. Luck.
Rapid developments.
Recreation. Festivities.

DOWNSIDE:
Quarrels. Doubt.
Domestic dispute.
Jealousy. Regret.

NINE OF WANDS

This card generally warns of unseen threats, whether in your personal life or at work. You will need all your skill and experience, developed over time, to effectively defend yourself from these. For this reason, the card sometimes suggests the need to suspend operations, take a break and reassess your situation; here, the goblin appears to do so by dancing in the air. On the Downside, you may encounter obstacles in your way, with attendant delays and even, in some cases, illness. Issues that seemed dormant may suddenly flare up again. It's important that you do not overstretch your resources and keep your eyes open for veiled attacks from anyone around you.

Goblin Whispers

UPSIDE:
Threats. Self-defence.
Reassessment.
Adjournment.
Estrangement.
Frustration. Stagnation.

DOWNSIDE:
Obstacles. Problems.
Delays. Bad luck.
Sluggishness. Illness.

TEN OF WANDS

The serious look on the face of the goblin here reminds us that there is a double edge to the Ten of Wands card. On the one hand, it refers to the carrying of burdens, to people bearing false witness against you and to any resulting injustices; on the other hand, it implies that if you can weather these storms you will reap the harvest and attain great rewards. On the Downside, this card is heavy with warnings of potential plots against you, of intrigue and hypocrisy, resulting in loss of earnings or an illness brought on by these attacks. So, in a reading, it can be useful to look at the surrounding cards to identify the help of friends who truly care for your wellbeing.

Goblin Whispers

UPSIDE:
Burdens. Treachery. Injustice. Cruelty. Travel. Harvest. Great reward.

DOWNSIDE:
Obstacles. Loss. Intrigue. Hypocrisy. Plotting. Lack of substance.

PORTER OF WANDS

The Goblin Porter of Wands is seen as the card of the follower — for example, the fan who copies the skill or knowledge of a person whom he or she admires without actually embodying it. Such people may offer to carry your burdens without truly understanding them, and perhaps expecting payment of some kind. On the Downside, the Goblin Porter can be a bringer of bad news and all his or her surface brilliance may be empty. It can be all too easy to find yourself falling under his spell, so you should be alert to any false or self-aggrandizing characteristics, which may be present in yourself as well as others, and which could lead you astray.

Goblin Whispers

UPSIDE:
Prodigy. Extraordinary.
Faithfulness. Emissary.
Supporter. Fan.

DOWNSIDE:
Falseness.
Powerlessness. Bad
news. Instability.
Faithlessness. Substance.

KNIGHT OF WANDS

The Goblin Knight of Wands proudly represents the spirit of an adventurer, the passion of a lover, the bravery of a soldier and the subtlety of a politician. In a reading, this card suggests that you are involved in an exciting project or significant enterprise, about which you can get carried away. You are probably someone who likes to be the centre of attention, but the excitement can cause you to make rash decisions and travel away from the road on which you began your journey. On the Downside, although you may enter *easily* into an exciting or romantic situation, you are likely to retreat when a deeper commitment is required — and your attempts to counteract this may lead to misunderstandings over which you have no control.

Goblin Whispers

UPSIDE:
Passion. Adventure. Subtlety. Journey. Moving into the unknown.

DOWNSIDE:
Disharmony. Evasion. Misunderstanding. Estrangement. Dissention. Unexpected changes. Abandonment.

LADY OF WANDS

The Goblin Lady of Wands is a powerful, kind and striking-looking leader, who is likely to have strong dramatic tendencies. If you encounter her you may find yourself carried along on the tide of her energy, knowledge and business acumen. She may also touch your heart with wonder. On the Downside, though, her theatricality can turn toward histrionics, and her golden touch can have somewhat of the extravagant about it. She can also be deceitful at times, so it's important to be careful in your dealings with both her and others.

Goblin Whispers

UPSIDE:
Feminine charm. Benevolence. Energy. Power. Business acumen. Sympathetic companion.

DOWNSIDE:
Drama. Theatricality. Extravagance. Deceit. Abandonment.

LORD OF WANDS

A teacher and visionary capable of inspiring everyone who encounters him, the Goblin Lord of Wands is usually a dazzling, quicksilver figure. Here, he holds the blackberry that is symbolic of the Wands suit between thumb and finger, as though about to eat it. In a reading, he often stands for a spiritual elder — one who can guide you on your journey, all the while keeping you safe. At his most powerful, he can represent incredible drive, ambition and intensity of achievement. On the Downside, he can be severe and full of anger — the kind of advisor whose words you do not wish to follow even though they may seem wise. And the fierceness and determination of his leadership can sometimes lead to reversals of fortune for those who follow him.

Goblin Whispers

UPSIDE:
Vision. Teaching. Leadership. Honesty. Generosity. Activity. Fierceness.

DOWNSIDE:
Severity. Anger. Bad or misleading advice. Lack of vision.

Wild Cards: The Sisters

The origin of the extra Wild Cards — also known as White Cards, *Cartes Blanches* or Significators — dates back to the 17th century, where they emerged amidst the development of cartomancy, from which tarot grew.

One story of origin goes that King Charles II, in flight from Cromwell's Roundheads, offered his supporters a blank (therefore "white") sheet of paper with his signature at the bottom. The recipient of this could then write anything they wanted above the royal signature and it would be considered legal — a linguistic meaning that the term "to give someone carte blanche" still has to this day.

This idea was picked up by early cartomancers, who saw it as a means of giving the person consulting the cards the option of a specific card to represent *them*. Over time, beginning with the 18th-century cartomancer Etteilla (1738–1791), the White Card began to act as a means of allowing the reading to shift focus. Either of these approaches can be applied to White Cards, or Wild Cards, today — as you will see in the pages that follow.

In traditional tarot, there is usually just a *single* Wild Card, but we have included two — to represent the two young heroines of the *Goblin Market* poem that inspired the deck, here simply called the Sisters.

We have entitled the cards "The One Who Went into Faery" and "The One Who Stayed Behind" — with each one representing a different set of qualities based on the action that she took in the poem.

Although they are not part of the traditional tarot sequence, the Sister cards can be used in two main ways:

1. As markers that help in the choice of a Significator that represents you, the reader. This is done by shuffling one of the two Sister cards into the deck, then leafing through the cards until you find the Sister. You choose the card either above or below the Sister as your Significator.

2. As a way of changing your personal approach to both the reading and the issue in hand – as suggested as a means to find a fifth card in the Four Fruits Spread on page 153. You could decide to make one of the sisters your Significator if you want – either by choosing randomly between them *or* by intentionally selecting the one you feel best represents the issue you are exploring, as per the option given in the Goblin Market Stall Spread on page 147. "The One Who Went into Faery" represents boldness and vision, but also rashness and trivialization of events; while "The One Who Stayed Behind" represents a more cautious approach, with a desire to place safety over pleasure.

We suggest that you explore and play with these Sister cards as much as you can, to get a sense of the way they might impact your readings.

The One Who Went into Faery

We hear a great deal about the sister who went into Faery in Christina Rossetti's enchanting poem – most of it negative. She is the sister who ignores the warnings of her sibling and accepts the dangerous fruit of the Goblin Market, with the negative consequences that ensue. Here, we see this sister surrounded by the goblins and their all-too-tempting wares. Essentially, the two sisters represent different approaches to life. This sister is seduced by the seemingly glamorous world of Faery, which might make her seem wild, thoughtless and reckless. However, this insight should be balanced with an appreciation of the clarity of vision, boldness and determination that it takes to choose to walk in enchanted lands, where there is the danger of getting lost in the coils of its wonders and enchantments.

THE ONE WHO STAYED BEHIND

Y ou would be forgiven
for seeing this sister
from Christina Rossetti's
remarkable poem as
someone who turns away
from the risks inherent in
visiting the Goblin Market
simply due to being ultra-
cautious. Yet we should not
forget that her caution is
driven by her own vision and
understanding. She does not simply
turn her back on the Faery realm; she sees it clearly as a
place that is both perilous *and* that offers the potential
for wisdom and change. Her capacity to see things in
this way affects her power over the goblins there, to the
extent that in the imagery of the card we see her *scattering*
the goblins and their fruits. Nor should we forget that in
the poem she continues to watch and wait for her sister
from outside, suggesting a strength of will that guards her
from rushing in; and also that in the end she *does* cross
the border between the worlds in order to bring her sister
home, suggesting both great loyalty and great courage.

THE CARD BACK

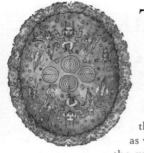

The image on the back of *The Goblin Market Tarot* cards evokes the magical, mysterious and often mischievous world of the Goblin Market, and the Faery realm on whose borders it lies. Filled with the goblins' tempting fruit, as well as symbols that guard the way between the human and faery worlds — especially the symbol of the Sidhe, which appears throughout the deck (see page 22) — it shows the energy and ebullience of the goblin faery host — dancing, laughing, tumbling, and turning around us, as we hold the cards in our hands.

PART 2

Working with *The Goblin Market Tarot*

*I*NTRODUCTION

Working with *The Goblin Market Tarot* can be revelatory. Even as we designed and wrote the deck, we were often amazed at how well they suited the archetypal resonances of traditional tarot. The mysterious and, at times, wickedly funny voice of Christina Rossetti's poem (see Part 3 / pages 169–189), echoed by the individual voices of the goblins, rang in our heads as we worked.

In the pages that follow, we offer a range of specifically designed sample spreads that you can try. These are:

- The Goblin Market Stall Spread
- The Four Fruits Spread
- The Goblin Market Exchange Spread
- Counting Out the Cards
- The Sisters Spread

However, you can, of course, use the Goblin Market deck in any way that you feel instinctively drawn to in order to seek help with issues, questions and decisions in your life, including using more traditional tarot spreads, or layouts, if you are familiar with them, as well as ways of working with the Wild cards.

THE GOBLIN MARKET STALL SPREAD

This spread is designed to open up the whole idea of the Goblin Market and the lore that lies within it. It involves laying out 12 cards based on the actual layout of a typical market – in two rows of "stalls" with the addition of a Significator (a card to represent you and your issue or question) at one end, plus a final, twelfth card that brings together the other elements of the reading at the other end.

Here is how it will look:

The Goblin Market Stall Spread

If you are used to laying out tarot cards in predetermined positions that include their own meanings, please note there are none in this spread.

1. To begin, simply shuffle the deck and either use whatever card comes to the top of the deck as a Significator to represent you and your enquiry, *or* use one of the Sisters to select a Significator; this can change the whole direction of the rest of the reading, according to which of the sisters enters the Faery realm.

2. Place your chosen Significator card face-up as shown in the diagram and then lay out ten further cards, face-down, in two rows of five as shown.

3. Select a final card and place this at the top of the two lines, also face-down, to represent the concluding aspect of the reading.

4. Then, to do the reading, turn over the two rows of cards, starting at "1" and criss-crossing between the two rows up to "10" — as if moving from stall to stall in an actual market. Read the cards in order, taking your time to study each one and consider how it relates to your question.

5. Finally, when you are satisfied that you have let each one tell its story and taken in all that you can, turn over the Conclusion card and see how this relates to the rest. This will be the end of your reading.

Sample Goblin Market Stall Reading

Here follows a sample Goblin Market Stall reading to show you how this spread works. The client in question wanted to know about a promotional opportunity in her life, which was complicated by the presence of a disaffected co-worker with whom she did not get on. What might it be best for her to do?

- First, she elected to draw **The One Who Went into Faery** as most suited not only to her personality, but also to the energy that she felt would be required to undertake the new job if she got the promotion.

The ten cards that she then drew from the deck were:

1: Ten of Wands	6: Three of Crowns
2: Ace of Wands	7: Four of Cups
3: Two of Cups	8: Knight of Platters
4: Ace of Crowns	9: Three of Wands
5: Ace of Platters	10: Lord of Wands

It was noticed immediately that there was a proliferation of wands in the reading: four, versus just two of each of the other three suits. This confirmed that the question was work-related.

- The first card, the **Ten of Wands**, spoke of bearing burdens and of having someone bear false witness. However, the implication was that if the storms were ridden out, great rewards could be had.
- The second card, the **Ace of Wands**, was seen as being all about good beginnings and a decree that it was hard to fail, whatever the enterprise entered into. This perfectly balanced the negative aspects of the previous card.
- The third card, the **Two of Cups** — concerned with love, harmony, attraction and partnership, as well as choice and two streams flowing together — clearly indicated that the two streams of the client's current job and the new one she was considering flowed into each other, and that the energy was one of harmony rather than stress.
- The fourth card, the **Ace of Crowns**, suggested the need for a strong boundary against disorder. This seemed to indicate that a boundary against the client's disaffected colleague would be necessary, but the card also suggested keeping a cool head without too much emotional input.
- The fifth card, the **Ace of Platters**, offered such a powerfully positive influence that it relinquished virtually any negativity present in the reading and pointed to general good fortune with an increase in pay. However, it also warned against resting on one's laurels.

- The sixth card, the **Three of Crowns**, immediately took the reading back into an area of disharmony. The underlying meaning of breaking apart could be seen as a possible danger after the client's departure from one job for another. However, the overwhelmingly positive aspects of the Ace of Platters, paired opposite it, seemed to mitigate this. The card also spoke of working through this difficulty.

- The seventh card, the **Four of Cups**, focused on a feeling of weariness and dissatisfaction at work, with a suggested solution of stepping aside, resting and keeping clear of ill-will or bitterness toward others.

- The eighth card, the **Knight of Platters**, indicated the presence of a powerful ally, especially at a time of challenge. This could either be the client's own inner strength, or that of another, but here she felt that her possible new boss might be a less positive supporter.

- The ninth card, the **Three of Wands** — representative of action and movement into a new dimension as well as looking for people who will support you — encouraged the client to be bold and courageous, with an expectation for her enterprise to move toward success.

- The tenth card, the **Lord of Wands** — who presents a dazzling figure, capable of inspiring everyone around him — reminded the client of her drive, ambition and desire for achievement.

Thus far the balance of the reading suggested that there were many positive aspects to the client's potential job change, despite a degree of opposition which seemed manageable.

- The client then turned over the eleventh card (the Conclusion card) that she had drawn — only to find the **Porter of Wands**, who can be seen as leading people astray at times while at the same time praising everything they do. The client at once recognized this as potentially representing the person who would be her new boss if she chose to accept the post. As a result, she revised the whole reading, coming to the conclusion that, despite the positive aspects throughout, the upshot of going for a promotion would set her against her colleague and place her under the leadership of someone who could be difficult and possibly lead her astray.

From this, we later learned that she decided to remain in her present post at that time, but shortly after was promoted to a different position which better suited her qualities and needs.

The Four Fruits Spread

Given the importance of fruits both in Christina Rossetti's *Goblin Market* poem and the way we have assigned a particular fruit to each suit in *The Goblin Market Tarot*, below is a reading that focuses on these fruits.

This is a decision-focused spread, offering four paths to take toward whatever goal you are seeking.

1. To make the reading, first pull all the Minor Arcana cards from the deck and sort them into their suits. Then shuffle each mini deck and lay them in four face-down piles.
2. Consider the question you want to address and then draw a card from the top of each of the four decks, laying them out as below — in the four cardinal directions of North, East, South and West, with a card from each suit for each one.

   1. Crowns — Apples — North
   2. Cups — Strawberries — East
   3. Platters — Pears — South
   4. Wands — Blackberries — West

3. Read the cards in turn, considering the implications of each one as regards the decision you have to make.

4. If you find that no single card is giving you a clear answer, you can draw a fifth card to help you if desired. To do this, either choose a card at random from the Major Arcana, place it in the centre, and use this to clarify any one of the original four cards in the spread – or choose one of the Sister Wild Cards, shuffle her randomly into the deck and then draw, as the fifth card in your reading, whichever card lies above the Sister when holding the deck face-up.

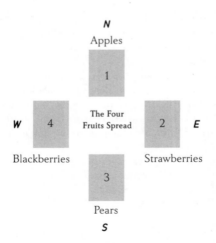

N

Apples

1

W | 4 | The Four Fruits Spread | 2 | **E**

Blackberries

Strawberries

3

Pears

S

Sample Four Fruits Reading

Here follows a sample Four Fruits reading to show you how this spread works. The client in question was thinking of setting up an online store to sell handmade wares. There were several options open to him and he sought the advice of *The Goblin Market Tarot* as this was clearly involved with trading and commerce.

When he turned his four cards over, he found that he had:

- **North: Ace of Crowns (Apples)**
  The Suit of Crowns is all about ideas, planning and execution, with the most important aspect of the Ace being the strength that it holds, and the apples being linked to luck and protection. The Ace of Crowns represents everything that a crown brings with it — purpose, dedication and leadership, as well as a need for an intellectual, rather than an emotional, response — and a stripping away of old ideas to get to the truth.

  The appearance of this card therefore seemed positive to the client, suggesting that his enterprise would be strong and safe from attack or loss, and reminding him of the dedication that he had already tapped into in order to come as far as he had with his ideas. However, it also made him realize that he might need to reconsider some of his older ideas as being less relevant in the present time.

- **East: Seven of Cups (Strawberries)**

  The Suit of Cups is about love, home and family. The fact that the Seven of Cups is known as a card for dreamers who fashion wonderful castles from clouds that may soon melt way alerted the client to be careful not to become too enraptured by his own plans, while the suit's asociation with family suggested that he should be clear how his enterprise would affect those close to him. The client also saw the appearance of this card as a warning against becoming too wrapped up in the creation of his dreams and perhaps not paying enough attention to the business side of things.

- **South: Two of Platters (Pears)**

  The Suit of Platters is all about gain, and pears are seen as the gift of the gods — helpful to ward off sickness and despair. Although the essential meaning of the Two of Platters is hindrance, distraction and worry, paradoxically its interpretation focuses on the success and wealth that grows out of the fantastic energy of the Ace of Platters, reminding us that once success and wealth are achieved, they require time and attention to be sustained.

  The client saw the appearance of this card as a sign of problems that had already raised their heads in his business plan. He felt that he was being asked to consider whether he had the stamina to proceed despite these potential problems, knowing that if he did, he would have powerful protection behind him.

- **West: Nine of Wands (Blackberries)**
  The Suit of Wands is very much concerned with enterprise; the Nine generally warns against unseen threats, whether at home or at work; and blackberries can have prickly associations. The indication of the Nine of Wands in particular is that you may need to use every ounce of your skill and experience, developed over time, to defend an idea. For this reason, the card sometimes suggests the need to suspend operations, to take a break and to reassess the situation.

  This the client saw as a warning against rivals who were offering similar goods to his own. Should he wait and take a more measured approach to his fledgling business?

- **Fifth Card**
  Each of the four cards provided him with valuable insight and had a strong bearing on his plans. However, he decided to draw a fifth card – from the Major Arcana – to help anchor the reading. He drew the **Faery Wanderer**, which he saw as representing himself and his aspirations. The Faery Wanderer had the courage to step off into space, trusting his vision

and following the mysterious path before him. The client saw this card as a sign that he had to trust that his vision and determination would carry him through as long as he took sensible precautions against being misled or attacked by rivals.

We heard later that he had taken the plunge with his new business and that it had got off to a fantastic start.

Note: Don't forget to shuffle the deck thoroughly after working with this spread, to ensure that the suits and majors are properly randomized.

THE GOBLIN MARKET EXCHANGE SPREAD

This simple spread, which involves the seeker simply drawing two cards at random from the shuffled deck, brings its user to the heart of the kind of "exchange" that takes place at the Goblin Market — with the first card representing the deck user's wish and the second card representing the faery, or goblin, response to this.

Throughout the lore of Faery, the theme of exchange occurs again and again. Faeries offer rewards for a price; in the darker stories, this can be as serious as their lives or their place in the community. When the person challenged stands firm and meets the faery head on, the results can be extraordinary. In the same way, buying something from the Goblin Market is, of course, a kind of exchange that can be beneficial. However, take care when you chose to make exchanges with the faery race, as they will hold you to any promises you make, come what may.

Sample Goblin Market Exchange Reading

Here follows a sample Goblin Market Exchange reading to show you howw this spread works. In this case, the client in question sought blessing for a new enterprise he was about to begin. What help could the goblins offer? The two cards that he drew were:

1. **The Eight of Cups (the client's wish)**
The essence of this card is uncertainty and disappointment, with a suggestion of the need to think again. The fact that the goblin on the card sees only his own face reflected, suggested to the client that his idea might lead nowhere.

2. **The Ten of Wands (the faery response)**
As this card is mostly about burdens and injustice, initially the client could only see its appearance as negative. But when he looked for longer, he began to understand the subtlety of the goblin wisdom, realizing that if he pushed ahead, past the difficulties of *launching* his new enterprise, the rewards were likely to be good. From this, he saw that the negative aspect of his wish card was actually his own self-doubt reflected back at him from previous failures, and the sense of struggle that seemed to be foretold therefore caused him to feel even more determined.

He decided to take the chance and push ahead with his idea; we were happy to hear that it was an overall success.

You will see from this sample reading that the answers are not always immediately positive, or indeed understandable. In most instances where we have used this spread, we have advised the client to take substantial time to really study the possible meanings, rather than to rush ahead. As with all Faery magic, there are many ways to read the answers — and not all are obvious.

COUNTING OUT THE CARDS

Another way of doing a reading with the Goblin Market deck is known as Counting Out.

Option 1

One approach to Counting Out the Cards is to shuffle the deck and then lay the cards down from the new top of the deck one at time, while saying aloud: "Ace, 2, 3, 4, 5, 6, 7, 8, 9, 10, Porter, Knight, Lady, Lord ... "

Whenever you say a number, for example 5, and at the same time the card you are laying down is a 5 of one of the suits, set that aside — ignoring the Majors as you do this. By the time you have counted out the whole deck you should have a small number of cards set aside. (If you end up with none — although this rarely happens — simply continue cycling through the deck until you have a separate stack of cards.)

Then simply read the cards that have ended up in this

separate stack one by one, in the order you laid them down, as if you were telling a story.

Option 2

An alternative approach to Counting Out the Cards is to use a Counting Out chant, instead of the "Ace, 1, 2, 3, 4..." approach above, while laying down the cards.

Here, you start laying the cards from the top of the deck down one at time, while saying aloud the following chant, or rhyme:

Blackberries, Strawberries, Apples and Pears,
1 2 3 4 5 – come buy our wares.
6 7 8 9 10 – Porter, Knight, Lady and Lord,
Luscious and lovely for all to afford.

As you say the first line, set aside any fruit card from the Minor Arcana that you come across in your laying down.

Then, as you continue the rhyme, set aside any number card or court card that you happen to be laying down at the same time you are saying its name.

As in the first counting-out approach above, you then just read the story told by the cards that end up set aside – in the order that you set them aside.

THE SISTERS SPREAD

As explained on page 140 where you first encountered the Sister Wild Cards, their main purpose is either to act as markers to help find a Significator when shuffled into the deck, or to change the overall meaning of a reading, potentially even by one of them being a Significator in their own right.

However, here follows an example of how to use the Sister cards in a way that constitutes a full reading in itself.

1. When you have an issue upon which you need advice, shuffle both the Sisters into the deck while thinking of your situation.
2. Turn the deck face-up in your hands and look through it. When you find the Sisters, pull them up but do not remove them from the deck.
3. Check to see which two cards are on either side of each Sister card and pull out each pair.
4. Place the two cards that were on either side of **The One Who Went into Faery** in one pile, remembering that she is the bolder and more impulsive of the two sisters. And keep the two cards that were on either side of **The One Who Stayed Behind** in another pile, remembering that she is the more thoughtful and cautious of the two.

5. Then do a reading of each pair of cards from the point of view of each Sister — seeing how the two cards affect each other in each instance. And consider which advice feels best for you.

Sample Sister Spread Reading

Here follows a sample reading of the Sisters Spread for clients who were considering moving to a new house. They had already looked at several properties, ranging from ones in more built-up areas to those further out, but they couldn't agree on which was most suitable for them and their growing family.

Reading with The One Who Went into Faery

They found the **Five of Cups** and the **Ace of Cups** on either side of **The One Who Went into Faery**.

- The **Five of Cups** tends to offer rather a bleak message. However, as well as recognizing this, my clients were careful to remember that beneath this grim foretelling there can often lie a major turning point — a moment when the correct decision can mean everything.
- Looking next at the **Ace of Cups**, which represents home life, family, fertility and generosity of spirit, they read the person normally represented by the card to stand for the potential new house and felt that this was a sign of it being associated

with good spirit and love. Since this is also a card of good omens, they felt the new home would flourish and grow.

Reading with The One Who Stayed Behind
They found the **Two of Wands** and the **Eight of Crowns** on either side of **The One Who Stayed Behind**.

- The **Two of Wands** generally indicates sadness, anger and a quarrelsome situation. However, as well as recognizing this, my clients were careful to remember that it can also stand for new possibilities and close friends.
- Looking next at the **Eight of Crowns**, which generally represents being tied down and unable to move, the clients thought of possible delays due to chains of buyers. But they also wondered if they might be holding *themselves* back and whether, if they could push past the initial stages, they might be able to find a way forward.

All in all, while they saw the importance of courageously moving ahead, they felt warned by the cards that they might be better off taking longer to decide and acting more cautiously, as per the sister who stayed behind in the poem, taking full stock of things before acting. When last heard, they were still in their old home but on the look-out for the right place to move to when the time is right.

However you choose
to work with *The Goblin Market
Tarot*, we are sure that you will have
a wild ride and find deep, helpful
answers to your questions and issues.
We hope that you enjoy the company
of the goblins and faeries as much
as we have enjoyed bringing
them to you, and that the
wisdom of Faery will help
to change your view
of the world around you.

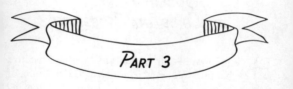

PART 3

The Poem
that Inspired
the Deck

GOBLIN MARKET
BY CHRISTINA ROSSETTI

H ere follows the full version of Christina Rossetti's enchanting *Goblin Market* poem. The meaning of this is discussed in the first part of this book, and many others can be found. It is a remarkable work, which acknowledges the two sides of the faery realms, both light and shadow - but it should be remembered that it was written during the Victorian era, in which many ideas that have since vanished or been modified were present. It is also, for many, perhaps overly sentimental. We suggest you read it with care and allow its magic to infuse you as you work with the cards.

Goblin Market

Morning and evening
Maids heard the goblins cry:
"Come buy our orchard fruits,
Come buy, come buy:
Apples and quinces,
Lemons and oranges,
Plump unpeck'd cherries,
Melons and raspberries,
Bloom-down-cheek'd peaches,
Swart-headed mulberries,
Wild free-born cranberries,
Crab-apples, dewberries,
Pine-apples, blackberries,
Apricots, strawberries;—
All ripe together
In summer weather,—
Morns that pass by,
Fair eves that fly;
Come buy, come buy:
Our grapes fresh from the vine,
Pomegranates full and fine,
Dates and sharp bullaces,
Rare pears and greengages,
Damsons and bilberries,
Taste them and try:
Currants and gooseberries,

Bright-fire-like barberries,
Figs to fill your mouth,
Citrons from the South,
Sweet to tongue and sound to eye;
Come buy, come buy."

Evening by evening
Among the brookside rushes,
Laura bow'd her head to hear,
Lizzie veil'd her blushes:
Crouching close together
In the cooling weather,
With clasping arms and cautioning lips,
With tingling cheeks and finger tips.
"Lie close," Laura said,
Pricking up her golden head:
"We must not look at goblin men,
We must not buy their fruits:
Who knows upon what soil they fed
Their hungry thirsty roots?"
"Come buy," call the goblins
Hobbling down the glen.

"Oh," cried Lizzie, "Laura, Laura,
You should not peep at goblin men."
Lizzie cover'd up her eyes,
Cover'd close lest they should look;
Laura rear'd her glossy head,
And whisper'd like the restless brook:

"Look, Lizzie, look, Lizzie,
Down the glen tramp little men.
One hauls a basket,
One bears a plate,
One lugs a golden dish
Of many pounds weight.
How fair the vine must grow
Whose grapes are so luscious;
How warm the wind must blow
Through those fruit bushes."
"No," said Lizzie, "No, no, no;
Their offers should not charm us,
Their evil gifts would harm us."
She thrust a dimpled finger
In each ear, shut eyes and ran:
Curious Laura chose to linger
Wondering at each merchant man.
One had a cat's face,
One whisk'd a tail,
One tramp'd at a rat's pace,
One crawl'd like a snail,
One like a wombat prowl'd obtuse and furry,
One like a ratel tumbled hurry skurry.
She heard a voice like voice of doves
Cooing all together:
They sounded kind and full of loves
In the pleasant weather.

Laura stretch'd her gleaming neck
Like a rush-imbedded swan,
Like a lily from the beck,
Like a moonlit poplar branch,
Like a vessel at the launch
When its last restraint is gone.

Backwards up the mossy glen
Turn'd and troop'd the goblin men,
With their shrill repeated cry,
"Come buy, come buy."
When they reach'd where Laura was
They stood stock still upon the moss,
Leering at each other,
Brother with queer brother;
Signalling each other,
Brother with sly brother.
One set his basket down,
One rear'd his plate;
One began to weave a crown
Of tendrils, leaves, and rough nuts brown
(Men sell not such in any town);
One heav'd the golden weight
Of dish and fruit to offer her:
"Come buy, come buy," was still their cry.
Laura stared but did not stir,
Long'd but had no money:
The whisk-tail'd merchant bade her taste
In tones as smooth as honey,

The cat-faced purr'd,
The rat-faced spoke a word
Of welcome, and the snail-paced even was heard;
One parrot-voiced and jolly
Cried "Pretty Goblin" still for "Pretty Polly;"—
One whistled like a bird.

But sweet-tooth Laura spoke in haste:
"Good folk, I have no coin;
To take were to purloin:
I have no copper in my purse,
I have no silver either,
And all my gold is on the furze
That shakes in windy weather
Above the rusty heather."
"You have much gold upon your head,"
They answer'd all together:
"Buy from us with a golden curl."
She clipp'd a precious golden lock,
She dropp'd a tear more rare than pearl,
Then suck'd their fruit globes fair or red:
Sweeter than honey from the rock,
Stronger than man-rejoicing wine,
Clearer than water flow'd that juice;
She never tasted such before,
How should it cloy with length of use?
She suck'd and suck'd and suck'd the more
Fruits which that unknown orchard bore;
She suck'd until her lips were sore;

Then flung the emptied rinds away
But gather'd up one kernel stone,
And knew not was it night or day
As she turn'd home alone.

Lizzie met her at the gate
Full of wise upbraidings:
"Dear, you should not stay so late,
Twilight is not good for maidens;
Should not loiter in the glen
In the haunts of goblin men.
Do you not remember Jeanie,
How she met them in the moonlight,
Took their gifts both choice and many,
Ate their fruits and wore their flowers
Pluck'd from bowers
Where summer ripens at all hours?
But ever in the noonlight
She pined and pined away;
Sought them by night and day,
Found them no more, but dwindled and grew grey;
Then fell with the first snow,
While to this day no grass will grow
Where she lies low:
I planted daisies there a year ago
That never blow.
You should not loiter so."
"Nay, hush," said Laura:
"Nay, hush, my sister:

I ate and ate my fill,
Yet my mouth waters still;
To-morrow night I will
Buy more;" and kiss'd her:
"Have done with sorrow;
I'll bring you plums to-morrow
Fresh on their mother twigs,
Cherries worth getting;
You cannot think what figs
My teeth have met in,
What melons icy-cold
Piled on a dish of gold
Too huge for me to hold,
What peaches with a velvet nap,
Pellucid grapes without one seed:
Odorous indeed must be the mead
Whereon they grow, and pure the wave they drink
With lilies at the brink,
And sugar-sweet their sap."

Golden head by golden head,
Like two pigeons in one nest
Folded in each other's wings,
They lay down in their curtain'd bed:
Like two blossoms on one stem,
Like two flakes of new-fall'n snow,
Like two wands of ivory
Tipp'd with gold for awful kings.
Moon and stars gaz'd in at them,

Wind sang to them lullaby,
Lumbering owls forbore to fly,
Not a bat flapp'd to and fro
Round their rest:
Cheek to cheek and breast to breast
Lock'd together in one nest.

Early in the morning
When the first cock crow'd his warning,
Neat like bees, as sweet and busy,
Laura rose with Lizzie:
Fetch'd in honey, milk'd the cows,
Air'd and set to rights the house,
Kneaded cakes of whitest wheat,
Cakes for dainty mouths to eat,
Next churn'd butter, whipp'd up cream,
Fed their poultry, sat and sew'd;
Talk'd as modest maidens should:
Lizzie with an open heart,
Laura in an absent dream,
One content, one sick in part;
One warbling for the mere bright day's delight,
One longing for the night.

At length slow evening came:
They went with pitchers to the reedy brook;
Lizzie most placid in her look,
Laura most like a leaping flame.
They drew the gurgling water from its deep;

Lizzie pluck'd purple and rich golden flags,
Then turning homeward said: "The sunset flushes
Those furthest loftiest crags;
Come, Laura, not another maiden lags.
No wilful squirrel wags,
The beasts and birds are fast asleep."
But Laura loiter'd still among the rushes
And said the bank was steep.

And said the hour was early still
The dew not fall'n, the wind not chill;
Listening ever, but not catching
The customary cry,
"Come buy, come buy,"
With its iterated jingle
Of sugar-baited words:
Not for all her watching
Once discerning even one goblin
Racing, whisking, tumbling, hobbling;
Let alone the herds
That used to tramp along the glen,
In groups or single,
Of brisk fruit-merchant men.

Till Lizzie urged, "O Laura, come;
I hear the fruit-call but I dare not look:
You should not loiter longer at this brook:
Come with me home.
The stars rise, the moon bends her arc,

Each glowworm winks her spark,
Let us get home before the night grows dark:
For clouds may gather
Though this is summer weather,
Put out the lights and drench us through;
Then if we lost our way what should we do?"

Laura turn'd cold as stone
To find her sister heard that cry alone,
That goblin cry,
"Come buy our fruits, come buy."
Must she then buy no more such dainty fruit?
Must she no more such succous pasture find,
Gone deaf and blind?
Her tree of life droop'd from the root:
She said not one word in her heart's sore ache;
But peering thro' the dimness, nought discerning,
Trudg'd home, her pitcher dripping all the way;
So crept to bed, and lay
Silent till Lizzie slept;
Then sat up in a passionate yearning,
And gnash'd her teeth for baulk'd desire, and wept
As if her heart would break.

Day after day, night after night,
Laura kept watch in vain
In sullen silence of exceeding pain.
She never caught again the goblin cry:
"Come buy, come buy;"—

She never spied the goblin men
Hawking their fruits along the glen:
But when the noon wax'd bright
Her hair grew thin and grey;
She dwindled, as the fair full moon doth turn
To swift decay and burn
Her fire away.

One day remembering her kernel-stone
She set it by a wall that faced the south;
Dew'd it with tears, hoped for a root,
Watch'd for a waxing shoot,
But there came none;
It never saw the sun,
It never felt the trickling moisture run:
While with sunk eyes and faded mouth
She dream'd of melons, as a traveller sees
False waves in desert drouth
With shade of leaf-crown'd trees,
And burns the thirstier in the sandful breeze.

She no more swept the house,
Tended the fowls or cows,
Fetch'd honey, kneaded cakes of wheat,
Brought water from the brook:
But sat down listless in the chimney-nook
And would not eat.

Tender Lizzie could not bear
To watch her sister's cankerous care
Yet not to share.
She night and morning
Caught the goblins' cry:
"Come buy our orchard fruits,
Come buy, come buy;"—
Beside the brook, along the glen,
She heard the tramp of goblin men,
The yoke and stir
Poor Laura could not hear;
Long'd to buy fruit to comfort her,
But fear'd to pay too dear.
She thought of Jeanie in her grave,
Who should have been a bride;
But who for joys brides hope to have
Fell sick and died
In her gay prime,
In earliest winter time
With the first glazing rime,
With the first snow-fall of crisp winter time.

Till Laura dwindling
Seem'd knocking at Death's door:
Then Lizzie weigh'd no more
Better and worse;
But put a silver penny in her purse,
Kiss'd Laura, cross'd the heath with clumps of furze
At twilight, halted by the brook:

And for the first time in her life
Began to listen and look.
Laugh'd every goblin
When they spied her peeping:
Came towards her hobbling,
Flying, running, leaping,
Puffing and blowing,
Chuckling, clapping, crowing,
Clucking and gobbling,
Mopping and mowing,
Full of airs and graces,
Pulling wry faces,
Demure grimaces,
Cat-like and rat-like,
Ratel- and wombat-like,
Snail-paced in a hurry,
Parrot-voiced and whistler,
Helter skelter, hurry skurry,
Chattering like magpies,
Fluttering like pigeons,
Gliding like fishes,—
Hugg'd her and kiss'd her:
Squeez'd and caress'd her:
Stretch'd up their dishes,
Panniers, and plates:
"Look at our apples
Russet and dun,
Bob at our cherries,
Bite at our peaches,

Citrons and dates,
Grapes for the asking,
Pears red with basking
Out in the sun,
Plums on their twigs;
Pluck them and suck them,
Pomegranates, figs."—

"Good folk," said Lizzie,
Mindful of Jeanie:
"Give me much and many: —
Held out her apron,
Toss'd them her penny.
"Nay, take a seat with us,
Honour and eat with us,"
They answer'd grinning:
"Our feast is but beginning.
Night yet is early,
Warm and dew-pearly,
Wakeful and starry:
Such fruits as these
No man can carry:
Half their bloom would fly,
Half their dew would dry,
Half their flavour would pass by.
Sit down and feast with us,
Be welcome guest with us,
Cheer you and rest with us."—
"Thank you," said Lizzie: "But one waits

At home alone for me:
So without further parleying,
If you will not sell me any
Of your fruits though much and many,
Give me back my silver penny
I toss'd you for a fee."—
They began to scratch their pates,
No longer wagging, purring,
But visibly demurring,
Grunting and snarling.
One call'd her proud,
Cross-grain'd, uncivil;
Their tones wax'd loud,
Their looks were evil.
Lashing their tails
They trod and hustled her,
Elbow'd and jostled her,
Claw'd with their nails,
Barking, mewing, hissing, mocking,
Tore her gown and soil'd her stocking,
Twitch'd her hair out by the roots,
Stamp'd upon her tender feet,
Held her hands and squeez'd their fruits
Against her mouth to make her eat.

White and golden Lizzie stood,
Like a lily in a flood,—
Like a rock of blue-vein'd stone
Lash'd by tides obstreperously,—

Like a beacon left alone
In a hoary roaring sea,
Sending up a golden fire,—
Like a fruit-crown'd orange-tree
White with blossoms honey-sweet
Sore beset by wasp and bee,—
Like a royal virgin town
Topp'd with gilded dome and spire
Close beleaguer'd by a fleet
Mad to tug her standard down.

One may lead a horse to water,
Twenty cannot make him drink.
Though the goblins cuff'd and caught her,
Coax'd and fought her,
Bullied and besought her,
Scratch'd her, pinch'd her black as ink,
Kick'd and knock'd her,
Maul'd and mock'd her,
Lizzie utter'd not a word;
Would not open lip from lip
Lest they should cram a mouthful in:
But laugh'd in heart to feel the drip
Of juice that syrupp'd all her face,
And lodg'd in dimples of her chin,
And streak'd her neck which quaked like curd.
At last the evil people,
Worn out by her resistance,
Flung back her penny, kick'd their fruit

Along whichever road they took,
Not leaving root or stone or shoot;
Some writh'd into the ground,
Some div'd into the brook
With ring and ripple,
Some scudded on the gale without a sound,
Some vanish'd in the distance.

In a smart, ache, tingle,
Lizzie went her way;
Knew not was it night or day;
Sprang up the bank, tore thro' the furze,
Threaded copse and dingle,
And heard her penny jingle
Bouncing in her purse,—
Its bounce was music to her ear.
She ran and ran
As if she fear'd some goblin man
Dogg'd her with gibe or curse
Or something worse:
But not one goblin scurried after,
Nor was she prick'd by fear;
The kind heart made her windy-paced
That urged her home quite out of breath with haste
And inward laughter.
She cried, "Laura," up the garden,
"Did you miss me?
Come and kiss me.
Never mind my bruises,

Hug me, kiss me, suck my juices
Squeez'd from goblin fruits for you,
Goblin pulp and goblin dew.
Eat me, drink me, love me;
Laura, make much of me;
For your sake I have braved the glen
And had to do with goblin merchant men."

Laura started from her chair,
Flung her arms up in the air,
Clutch'd her hair:
"Lizzie, Lizzie, have you tasted
For my sake the fruit forbidden?
Must your light like mine be hidden,
Your young life like mine be wasted,
Undone in mine undoing,
And ruin'd in my ruin,
Thirsty, canker'd, goblin-ridden?"—
She clung about her sister,
Kiss'd and kiss'd and kiss'd her:
Tears once again
Refresh'd her shrunken eyes,
Dropping like rain
After long sultry drouth;
Shaking with aguish fear, and pain,
She kiss'd and kiss'd her with a hungry mouth.

Her lips began to scorch,
That juice was wormwood to her tongue,

She loath'd the feast:
Writhing as one possess'd she leap'd and sung,
Rent all her robe, and wrung
Her hands in lamentable haste,
And beat her breast.
Her locks stream'd like the torch
Borne by a racer at full speed,
Or like the mane of horses in their flight,
Or like an eagle when she stems the light
Straight toward the sun,
Or like a caged thing freed,
Or like a flying flag when armies run.

Swift fire spread through her veins, knock'd at her
    heart,
Met the fire smouldering there
And overbore its lesser flame;
She gorged on bitterness without a name:
Ah! fool, to choose such part
Of soul-consuming care!
Sense fail'd in the mortal strife:
Like the watch-tower of a town
Which an earthquake shatters down,
Like a lightning-stricken mast,
Like a wind-uprooted tree
Spun about,
Like a foam-topp'd waterspout
Cast down headlong in the sea,
She fell at last;

Pleasure past and anguish past,
Is it death or is it life?

Life out of death.
That night long Lizzie watch'd by her,
Counted her pulse's flagging stir,
Felt for her breath,
Held water to her lips, and cool'd her face
With tears and fanning leaves:
But when the first birds chirp'd about their eaves,
And early reapers plodded to the place
Of golden sheaves,
And dew-wet grass
Bow'd in the morning winds so brisk to pass,
And new buds with new day
Open'd of cup-like lilies on the stream,
Laura awoke as from a dream,
Laugh'd in the innocent old way,
Hugg'd Lizzie but not twice or thrice;
Her gleaming locks show'd not one thread of grey,
Her breath was sweet as May
And light danced in her eyes.

Days, weeks, months, years
Afterwards, when both were wives
With children of their own;
Their mother-hearts beset with fears,
Their lives bound up in tender lives;
Laura would call the little ones

And tell them of her early prime,
Those pleasant days long gone
Of not-returning time:
Would talk about the haunted glen,
The wicked, quaint fruit-merchant men,
Their fruits like honey to the throat
But poison in the blood;
(Men sell not such in any town):
Would tell them how her sister stood
In deadly peril to do her good,
And win the fiery antidote:
Then joining hands to little hands
Would bid them cling together,
"For there is no friend like a sister
In calm or stormy weather;
To cheer one on the tedious way,
To fetch one if one goes astray,
To lift one if one totters down,
To strengthen whilst one stands."

Resources and Further Reading

John and Caitlín Matthews offer courses, workshops books and recordings on a wide variety of mythic and visionary subjects, including the world of Faery. For news and announcements of ongoing programmes, go to *www. hallowquest.org.uk*.

John's series of books and oracles on the Sidhe (see below) — which tell you more about the mysterious Celtic symbol found throughout the Goblin Market deck — are available from all good suppliers, directly from the Hallowquest site above and online from the publisher, Lorian Press, at *www.lorianpress.com*:

The Sidhe: Wisdom from the Celtic Otherworld
The Sidhe Oracle of the Shining Moon
The Sidhe Oracle of the Fleeting Hare
The Sidhe Oracle of the Glorious Sun
The Sidhe Oracle of the Flowing Waters

Other books that you may find useful include:

Briggs, Katherine, *A Dictionary of Fairies*, Allen Lane, 1976
Kruse, John, *British Fairies*, Green Magic, 2017
Matthews, Caitlín, *Untold Tarot*, Schiffer, 2018
Matthews, John, *Faeryland*, Abrams, 2013
Matthews, John and Froud, Brian, *How to See Faeries*, Abrams, 2011
Morgan, Lee, *Sounds of Infinity*, Witches' Almanac, 2019

THE GOBLIN MARKET ALBUM

Goblin Market Music

Goblin Market Music is the Christina Rossetti poem abridged and adapted into a suite of seven songs, a fusion of folk/rock and progressive/rock curated and produced by Steeleye Span's Julian Littman, with fellow members and special guests — making, writing, playing and singing contributions to complement the tarot deck and book.

The album is available for download on all the usual platforms and as a CD from Watkins Books (19–21 Cecil Ct, Covent Garden, London, WC2N 4EZ), Atlantis Books (49A Museum St, Holborn, London, WC1A 1LY) and on the merchandise table at all Steeleye Span live shows.

ACKNOWLEDGEMENTS

To my amazing collaborator Charles Newington, who was able to get inside my head and draw exactly what I was seeing. To my wife Caitlín for all her support, the details on the life and world of Christina Rossetti, the Sisters Wild Card idea, the Counting-Out chant and the many other suggestions that made this a better book. To Julian Littman, Andrew "Spud" Sinclair, Liam Genockey, Roger Carey and Jessie May Smart of Steeleye Span, as well as all the rest of the amazing talent who wrote, performed and produced the concept album *Goblin Market Music*, adding another layer of wonder to this project. To all at Watkins Media for their sterling help, and for their enthusiasm throughout the process of bringing this deck to birth. And, last but by no means least, to the author of the most intriguing faery poem of all: Christina Rossetti herself.

J. M., Oxford, 2020